BETTER
BIGGER
BOLDER

How To Break the Profit Barrier.
Predictably.

ROSEMARY PAETOW AND BOB SHER

INDIE BOOKS
INTERNATIONAL

The Predictable Profitability System™ is a pending trademark of InStrategy Leadership Inc dba Think inStrategy.

ISBN-13: 978-1-957651-61-3
Library of Congress Control Number: 2023923202

Cover designed by Laura Duffy Design
Interior designed by Amit Dey

INDIE BOOKS INTERNATIONAL®, INC.
2511 WOODLANDS WAY
OCEANSIDE, CA 92054
www.indiebooksintl.com

CONTENTS

Appendix.................................. **115**

PREFACE

You can build a better team. You can eliminate the excuses in your organization. Your company can be consistently more profitable. Your company can fulfill on its big potential. You can have balance in your life.

The problem is your staff are not operating at maximum efficiency. Most likely they are solving the wrong problems. This leads to making decisions that do not support and promote the consistent growth of your company.

Our Philosophy

When entrepreneurs first start out the formula for success is simple: to grow all one needs to do is put in the right processes and do the right marketing and everything else will sort itself out. That is why most business owners think adding sales is the clear and obvious way to grow a business.

Smart entrepreneurs realize that the formula for growth must change once a business grows beyond three million dollars in sales or greater than twenty employees. They understand a more robust framework is needed to continue to succeed. That framework now must include a leadership team and a delivery system that can absorb 30-45 percent annual growth for the business to continue to prosper. Otherwise, they know that spending time and money to add sales becomes a waste of time. Why? If an organization cannot seamlessly onboard and deliver on its promise to consistently provide excellent service new customers will leave. It then becomes a very expensive proposition to keep replacing the 'same' customer over and over again. Worse, it demoralizes the staff when sales plateau. So, if adding sales is not the answer, then what is?

We studied the approach of very successful CEOs whose companies consistently produced the sales and profits they desired. By doing so they avoided the "sales plateau trap." Their solution: they built a better team who consistently produced *predictable* sales and profitability.

We turned what these CEOs did into a best practice that we call the Predictable Profitability System. This system not only promotes predictable profitability, it also mitigates the inherent business risk growth incurs.

Predictable
Profitability System™

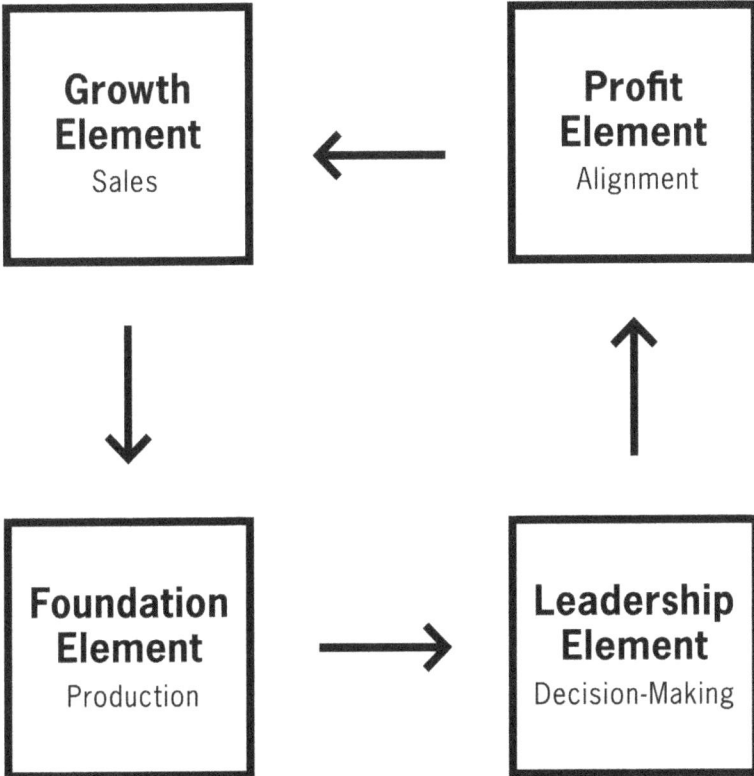

Growth Element Sales	**Profit Element** Alignment
↓	↑
Foundation Element Production →	**Leadership Element** Decision-Making

This system is organized around the framework that all businesses are built upon but it uses them differently. It consists of four elements: foundation, leadership, profitability, and growth. Here is a short description of each:

FOUNDATION

This element focuses on strengthening and stabilizing the platform upon which to consistently grow. Start here if you are having a churn of staff or clients.

LEADERSHIP

This element focuses on how to deliver the kind of feedback that improves performance. When culture (values + why), feedback, and rewards are aligned to what really matters to the business, consistent execution results. Start here if you have inconsistent revenue growth.

PROFIT

This element focuses on how to think in ways that deliver better decisions and better ideas, all designed to increase profitability. By incorporating a tool we call a "strategic lens," staff can more quickly identify the right problem to solve and develop better solutions. This results in greater efficiencies and profits. Start here if your net profit is too low.

GROWTH

This element focuses on what solution a company delivers to its customers that will best support predictable, consistent scalable growth (sales). To fulfill the business's true potential define that thing your company does best. Start here after all other elements have been fine-tuned to generate rapid growth.

Our Solution: The Predictable Profitability System

The objective of our Predictable Profitability System is to build a better, bigger company. That happens by doing two things.

First, build a better team. This doesn't mean getting rid of everyone and starting over. It means getting the existing team to work together as one unit. This eliminates excuses in a company and greatly reduces the number of problems or issues that need the CEO's immediate attention. In other words, building a better team creates high quality predictable performance which leads to staff engagement (and the natural elimination of poor performers).

Second, build genius thinking into a company's DNA. This new way of thinking allows a company to fulfill its potential by uncovering what it does best and can monetize. It creates a common strategic lens that staff use to ensure predictable profits and growth.

How long must you wait for results? Companies in Transition ($3-$12 million in revenue) typically take nine to twelve months of implementation to see noticeable changes in the top and bottom lines. Larger companies will see changes in six months or less. After that, 25 to 30 percent growth year over year is achievable.

Our objective is to help build Transition companies into growth machines that consistently and reliably generate their growth objectives year over year. Its net profitability tends to settle around 20 percent. Why is that important? It is the foundation for being bolder. People want to be part of something exciting, where they can grow their careers. Business owners want to experience success they can truly be proud of. Clients want to invest (pay you money) in something that provides excellent, elegant solutions.

Rosemary Paetow and Bob Sher
Think inStrategy
Carlsbad, CA
April, 2023

PART I

THE BARRIER TO BEING A BETTER, BIGGER, BOLDER COMPANY

1

WHY COMPANIES HIT THE BARRIER

*"My business is really poised to take
off...if only the pain of growth would stop
getting in my way."*

Anyone who has succeeded in business knows that point
where the success they enjoyed in the beginning stages of
building a company stops working. Double-digit growth stalls
while personnel issues climb. Silently the CEO thinks, "My
business is good—if only my people were better." A warning
light that something needs to change has just gone off. The
midsize[1] company has hit a growth barrier.

In our individual careers we witnessed this barrier play out
whenever an Emerging Firm attempted to become a Professionally Managed (PM)[2] firm. Pushing through it in our own
company, we discovered what breaks that barrier.

Coauthor Rosemary saw hints of it while working at KPMG,
one of the Big Four international accounting firms. Although
many of KPMG's clients are large institutions, like banks, they

also service a number of Emerging Firms. These young companies, less than five years old and typically under $10 million in revenue, are on a fast growth trajectory. Interestingly, they are organized and operate very differently from the well-established businesses typically being audited. As an auditor her job was to determine if these businesses had it in them to grow beyond $10 million. While some did, many did not.[3] And that got Rosemary very curious.

She expanded her research to bankers who worked with these small businesses (lending either working capital or assisting in asset purchases). They said they preferred to work with any business over $10 million as they were a "much safer investment" (translate that into more stable and reliable). Business valuation experts recommend anyone wanting to sell their company as an exit strategy should drive their company value past $10 million to have any kind of real return on a sale. It seems there is a definitive before and after $10 million in revenue relating to success.

While our stories measure success in terms of revenue or profit growth (it being the industry standard) the business executives we interviewed said it is the shift in the staff's perspective that made the real difference for them. They said when their staff aligned to the company why and culture and learned genius thinking, the company became fun. It is what the CEOs and leaders we interviewed for this book are most proud of: their people and the environment which was created as a result of this work. That is the kind of success we wrote this book to inspire.

Rosemary has had the privilege of working at and with some of the finest firms[4] San Diego has to offer. When she asked them about their growth experience, they admitted that their companies got stuck—and that breaking $10 million was the key to real business achievement. They confessed that they struggled with letting go of the day-to-day decision-making and with finding the best staff and keeping them motivated. When asked what the problem was, in hindsight, they blamed their revenue model for inconsistently producing sales. They noticed that the compulsion to add sales seemed to lead to some unintended consequences besides just a loss of profitability. In digging deeper what got them through has been incorporated into our new system of thinking.

Coauthor Bob discovered the same issues, and unintended consequences, at the organizations he supported.[5] There he saw division leaders and their strategic partners struggle with producing consistent, reliable results until they shifted their thinking. It started with increasing clarity and alignment for the teams. Then they could change from a production to a performance mentality. Once all that was in place the leader could tackle solving the right problems.

Together Rosemary and Bob have synthesized those unintended consequences into four easy-to-understand blunders and have created three tools to eliminate them and increase the odds of becoming a better, bigger, bolder leader and company.

Stories Of Midsize Company CEOs Who Got Better, Bigger, Bolder

In this book we focus on midsize company CEOs and their leadership teams who figured out how to be better, bigger, and bolder. While you could learn all this on your own, the stories and tools we will share can help you to avoid the common pitfalls (blunders) at this stage—or manage them faster if you are already there. You can save time, money, and frustration by using others' mistakes to turn your results around.

These stories apply to any leader who has financial responsibility for revenue or profit production, regardless of whether they are the business owner or not. As business researchers we recognize that while large companies have more complex decision-making events, they still used these tools for better decision-making. Becoming better, bigger, and bolder works for anyone who leads. It is based on how aligned the leader is to their business framework.

Meet Chen

A client introduced us to Chen, who wanted to break the $10 million growth barrier. Chen had taken his idea of a "smart-energy building" from nothing to a $4 million division within a well-known construction company. And yet, even with all his success, Chen was still struggling with the other division managers who would not listen to his suggestions to grow the entire organization. Chen's ideas for change were solid but he couldn't gain traction. He hadn't cracked the barrier, so he had not proven himself in their eyes. He was stuck.

He called us in to help him get unstuck. We told him it could be done, and it would require time and effort—Chen needed to change his belief that he had to solve all the problems (one of our four blunders). He also recognized that he and his management team needed to level up. Worse, their accounting and customer service systems were outdated and could not accommodate the kind of growth Chen wanted. He needed new software, better decision-makers and he needed to remove himself from the day-to-day operations, all while absorbing rapid growth. A tall order in a short timeframe.

There were some tough learning curves like creating a strategic lens for the team and changing his leadership element. In two years, revenue increased 2.5X and his entire existing team had leveled up. Best of all, Chen had proven he was an executive worthy of esteem.

Meet Diego

Diego, a new general manager, got a call from Brad, a VP at the corporate office, telling him, "We have a problem. If you don't increase your profits by at least 20 percent, you're out. I'm here to help if you need anything."

That's when Diego called us and said, "corporate gave me a mountain to climb. I've got the biggest budget I have ever managed, my profits are tanking, and I inherited a hostile culture of backstabbing and mistrust. Where do I start?"

Diego is the type of guy they make movies about. He was a troubled kid, running with gangs in high school, who joined the U.S. Navy to stay out of jail. After the Navy he found a job as an eight-dollar-per-hour laborer and worked his way up the ranks to become the general manager.

Where to start? Diego needed to change his mindset from an employee to a leader, build trust with a management team that does not trust any form of management, and produce predictable profitability. A big mountain to climb.

We started with addressing his leadership to build trust. We then helped align the team to a performance mindset, to drive profitability.

At the end of the year, Diego handed us his financials pointing to the bottom line. There was a 40 percent growth in profits—twice as much as Diego had envisioned. "But that's not the real victory," he said. "What really matters is my executive team grew into a better, cohesive team." The following year their revenue grew 160 percent.

This book will help you to recognize what gets you stuck (the barrier to better, bigger, bolder). You'll then learn how to get unstuck (the tools to better and bigger). And finally, we'll show you how to really accelerate using key concepts to change your game to bolder.

The Barrier Is Transition

Transition is defined as the process or a period of changing from one state or condition to another. We are introducing a new concept, the capitalized word *Transition*, that is the barrier to success.[6]

Transition with a capital T is a business phase in which an essential aspect of your framework needs to change and how you, as leader, think about how the business needs to change. The way you originally designed your business may now be up in the air. Even how you thought you would get there may be off the table. A leader can get stuck because what used to work, and should work, no longer does in this phase. To conquer Transition we will show you the red flags and the tools to change your perspective and your outcomes.

Two Kinds Of Transition

In our research, we have found a business will experience two types of Transitions. The first type happens when a company moves from an emerging firm to a professionally managed firm. If your revenue is between $3 million and $10 million your company is in Transition whether it seems like it or not. The first Transition is the hardest one to deal with because you haven't the experience yet to manage the paradoxes and noise.

Transition has you straddling the fence between an emerging firm and a professionally managed firm. You are no longer a solo practitioner with one or two staff, making all the key decisions. Yet, without a full management team, there are not enough staff to delegate tasks. Nor is there enough money to throw at the problems. Your time and attention are being pulled into solving multiple issues simultaneously.

This is the backdrop for Transition, being resource-starved in one, two, or all three critical areas of a business: staff, clients, and cash flow. This resource deprivation affects where one's focus goes and which problems are resolved, often dragging out the recovery process.

The second type of Transition occurs when a firm's revenue model (we call it the growth element) needs to change due an external economic factor. This impacts not only how the company makes money but also the new decisions it must now embrace to do so. So the growth element and the leadership element need to be upgraded. Usually, a company facing its second transition is well above $10 million in revenue.

In both cases the leadership body (not just the CEO) must newly define how they will manage and think.

The first Transition starts slowly—akin to a frog being heated in a pot of water—and causes all sorts of troubles. Staff just aren't humming along like they used to—productivity and therefore, profitability starts to suffer. The quality of output tanks. The harder you push for results the worse it seems to get. You may begin to experience staff burnout leading to greater staff turnover. And so you push even harder for more production to drive down costs while you try to figure out how to drive your revenue up (solving the wrong problem).

Now you have a cash flow crisis.

Elements of Success

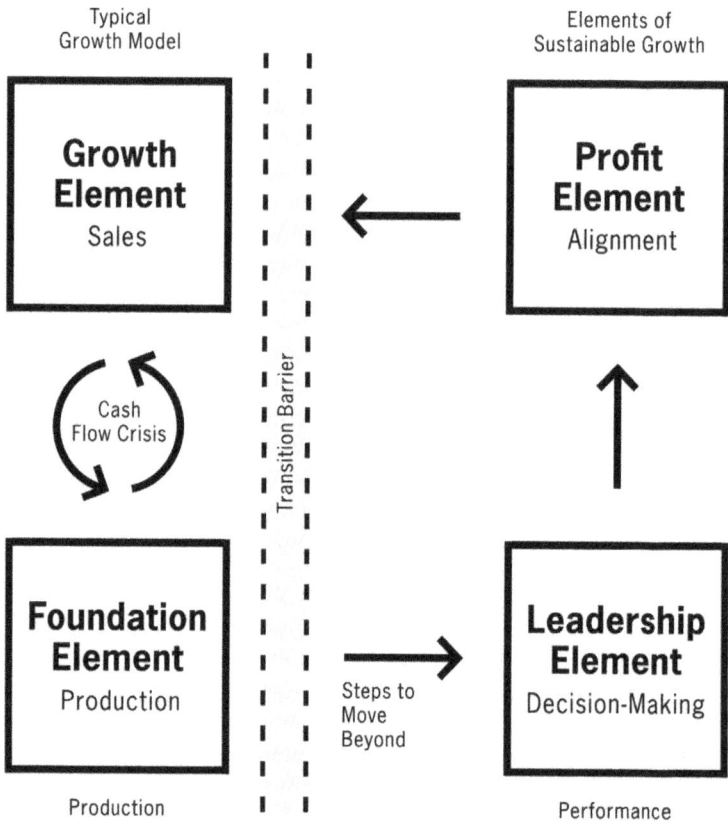

Typical
Growth Model

Elements of
Sustainable Growth

**Growth
Element**

Sales

**Profit
Element**

Alignment

Cash
Flow Crisis

Transition Barrier

**Foundation
Element**

Production

Steps to
Move
Beyond

**Leadership
Element**

Decision-Making

Production

Performance

How to break the transition barrier

The red flags indicating you are in Transition:

- Plateaued sales
- Metrics are not being met
- Your competitors are outstripping you
- Your passion is waning
- Lack of resources
- The four blunders (see below)

To alleviate these unwanted disruptions and getting stuck in a *Groundhog Day* drama, there are three essential tools we believe will help:

1. A system that increases the value of your firm not just the size
2. A method to promote productivity and profitability
3. A way of thinking and problem solving that sets your company apart—a new focus

Transition changes what the leader should focus on. Without having this awareness, most leaders in Transition typically fall prey to four blunders. These blunders chew up valuable resources, time, money, staff. Embedded in this is knowing the right problem to solve. Albert Einstein once suggested that the thinking that caused the 'problem' will not get you out of the problem. He suggested that new thinking, which encourages problems to be viewed differently, allows for brilliant solutions to emerge.

These Four Blunders Can Be Fatal

These blunders cause executives to stay stuck. Based on interviews with hundreds of business owners and division leaders, we identified four common blunders when their company transitioned from an emerging firm to a professionally managed firm. They said it delayed their growth because they focused on tactics (doing) rather than managing the big picture.

The blunders:

Blunder One: Thinking That Any Sale Is A Good Sale. Not all revenue is good revenue. Increasing revenue does not necessarily put more money in your bank account. It does, however, increase the potential for dissatisfied customers. Adding predictable, profitable revenue is needed to break the barrier.

Blunder Two: Settling For Who Is Available When Hiring. If you want a better, bigger, bolder business, you need staff willing to go the extra mile. While it may seem like you are hunting unicorns, what it really means is finding people aligned with your business framework. Clearly defining the framework and providing on-the-job training will support your leadership team when navigating through this barrier.

Blunder Three: Managing The Urgent Rather Than The Important. In business it has been said the tyranny of the urgent usually takes precedence over what is important. This results in executives working *in* the business rather than *on* the business. Success is hard to achieve if the focus is only on the next problem. Transition creates this trap by changing the focus of the CEO from big picture (strategy) to solving the day-to-day (tactics). A change in thinking—genius thinking—is needed.

Blunder Four: Over-relying On The Boss To Solve All Business Problems. Too often in the emerging stage a CEO falls prey to becoming the chief problem-solver because the problems seem to have multiplied. This is not a sustainable construct. A better, bigger, bolder business has many leaders who can solve the myriad of problems that arise consistently. When the CEO shifts from the chief problem-solver to the chief strategy designer, they develop and train staff to use a strategic lens that eliminates this blunder.

In Transition you might think more sales is the answer (blunder one) and you may find yourself settling for who is available when hiring (blunder two). As a result, you are now spending more of your time putting out fires than focusing on running the business (blunder three). Your reaction may be to jump back into the fray (blunder four) and put your rain-maker cape on in the hopes of generating more sales instead of addressing the issues that caused your sales to flatline in the first place. One major decision, leading to four cascading issues, all result in frustration and self-doubt—a loss of boldness.

The frustration and damage of Transition is expensive.

There Is No Secret Escape Hatch

Few people understand the unique pressures an executive faces in Transition. All of which can drain the leader of energy, clarity, and confidence. This time can feel like the land of the lacks: the lack of customers, time, money, and staff to execute. And yet it is also a highly creative time. An opportunity to do something new.

Every business owner who has taken their firm to the professionally managed stage has said it was worth the pain and their life is so much better now.

To become better, bigger, bolder you need new tools, new thinking.

Key Takeaways:

1. Transition is hard. A change in leading, thinking and finding solutions is needed. It often requires *solving two opposing problems* (a paradox) simultaneously.

2. The four blunders exacerbate and distract from the real problem the company is experiencing.

3. The red flags of Transition are:
   - Plateaued sales
   - Metrics are not being met
   - Your competitors are outstripping you
   - Your passion is waning
   - Lack of resources
   - The four blunders

2
HOW TO BREAK THE BARRIER

"Trying to solve all the problems you have will take too much time and money. Rather define a better system."

Entrepreneurs begin their journey with a big, shiny dream; a passion to do or create something meaningful. They have hope and excitement and in the beginning everything works. But along the way something happens. Somewhere, somehow the dream becomes a distant memory, and they are left with bickering, gossipy staff, and an endless stream of problems that seem like the whack-a-mole[7] game—handle one thing only to have two more show up. There is a gap between what they want the company to look like (a top performance organization) and how it is currently.

Transition has struck and brings with it a scarcity of resources: money, good staff, enough time. Worse it brings an abundance of problems like staff squabbling (or leaving) and managing cash flow. It is exhausting. You don't have enough of anything to solve the problem properly. And yet, if you do not solve them your company will shrink[8] maybe even die. As a result, many CEOs will drive harder on productivity and sales thinking it is the answer and yet it only triggers the four blunders.

Meet Harry

Harry is a successful attorney, running a mid-sized firm (twenty professional staff). He became an attorney because justice matters to him. It is what makes him a great litigator. Talk to anyone in town and they all recognize his name and know that if they meet him in court, it is likely that they will lose. Harry is a brilliant case strategist. He knows how to win.

But Harry is in a rut. And he is tired. He is tired of managing the minutia: all the staff issues and cashflow issues (For example, attorney's not submitting their billable hours timely, not collecting the money from clients promptly, and not understanding what his financials are really telling him). Harry is spending most of his time chasing money like an accountant and not being an attorney righting a wrong for his clients. He has fallen for blunder three (managing the urgent) and blunder four (chief problem solver).

Now his revenue has plateaued. He thinks the only way out is to demand more staff production. As Harry's firm lingers in Transition his staff begin to complain about stress and overwhelm. Worse, their projects aren't getting done or are being delivered late. Staff resent being assigned any more cases. Their reasoning: they already have too much on their plate while Harry thinks they are not working to capacity. Absenteeism, a lack of accountability, and cash flow issues have become a regular topic.

Have you ever tried to capitalize on your company's potential only to be inundated with so many more problems that it begins to look like you are climbing Mount Everest?

Harry was facing an endless number of glitches to solve and not getting traction in his firm, playing whack-a-mole managing the urgent rather than proactively planning and managing the important. The heartbreaking part: this is why so few companies grow beyond $10 million in revenue.

Harry said he wanted new tools and new thinking.

A New System To Take You To A Better Place

So, what will it really, truly take to be better, bigger, bolder? Getting into action will do that. But only if the actions taken are intentionally moving the company in the right direction. You need a system to help you rethink your business, to know where to start.

> The leaders in our proprietary research study have told us over and over again, when they reframe a problem a new and better solution presents itself. They call that genius thinking. Having a system to look at your business in its totality helps see connections that promote genius solutions.

If you want to stop being worn down, like Harry, by the day-to-day grind of having to make "stupid, meaningless decisions" (his words) you need better tools. It starts with understanding one's business framework.

Every business in existence has the following framework:

Framework	Building Block
How it delivers its solution to the customer	Foundation Element
Determines which actions produce the best results	Leadership Element
What will increase the company value	Profit Element
How to it intends to grow (revenue – USP*)	Growth Element

*Unique Selling Proposition

When a business owner starts out these are fairly simple, straightforward, and easy to understand elements. The growth element is simply how the firm makes money. What we sell and who buys from us. The leadership element is almost nonexistent because only the owner makes decisions. The foundation element is the infrastructure used to produce and deliver the product/service (processes, software systems, staff) of the company. The profit element is only revenue less costs to produce the revenue (its profit).

Transition changes all that. Now more than just a handful of folks are involved in the production and delivery of the product/service. Decisions are more complex and urgent. The CEO is no longer the leadership element. Profit is about more than just revenue minus direct costs. It is about problem solving, efficiencies, waste management, and more. Growth is no longer about just adding more customers. It is about creating predictable, consistent growth.

The Predictable Profitability System: A New Approach

Our Predictable Profitability System's new approach has two objectives.

First, build a better team. Second, build genius thinking into a company's DNA. This new way of thinking allows a company to fulfill on its potential by uncovering what it does best and can monetize. It creates a common strategic lens (way of thinking and solving problems) that staff use to ensure predictable profits and growth.

A Deeper Dive into the Components, Roles and Interplay of Each Element

The foundation element includes the infrastructure that delivers your product or service to the market. It incorporates your processes, your software/hardware and your staff. Ask yourself what needs to change in your infrastructure to be able to absorb accelerated growth?

The leadership element includes how management leads through performance and feedback. It includes the tools of culture and its strategic lens. Ask yourself how engaged are your staff? How excited are they to work at your company?

The profit element defines the rate of growth potential for a business. How a company thinks, what problems to solve and how to solve them differently, determines its efficiency and its effectiveness in growing to the next level. Ask yourself, are you as profitable as you think you should be?

The growth element defines the rate at which a company can change and absorb scalable *growth*. It includes what the company currently sells and what it could offer that is something unique and the market will pay top dollar for. Ask yourself, have you identified that 'thing' you are best at and that the market is craving?

The Predictable Profitability System can also be used to see the interplay between the elements.

The foundation-growth relationship determines the rate of potential your firm has. In other words, the degree to which your company is ready to scale and be profitable. Ask yourself: what is your close ratio with potential customers? Measure your market pull effectiveness by assessing how many prospects find you versus you looking for them. Ask yourself what your customer service is being used for: enhancement or reparation of reputation?

The leadership-profit relationship measures the alignment of the leadership body's decision-making skills, their effectiveness in producing the intended results on time and if they find Genius thinking that results in creative solutions. Ask yourself if your staff consistently deliver excellence? How well does your culture support your big ideas?

The foundation-leadership relationship predicts the potential business risk. Ask yourself if your staff arrive at the same or nearly the same decisions you would? Are they thinking of and implementing processes that shore up how the company delivers its product or service?

The profit -growth element relationship forecasts the consistency of performance and the predictability of your results. Ask yourself if you regularly meet or exceed revenue and profit goals?

Better. Bigger. Bolder.

Why better? Better is all about having a foundation that supports scalable growth *and* a leadership body aligned to execute on that growth. Our most successful clients said when they fine-tuned their process and developed and trained their staff with a company strategic lens they saw better decisions, better productivity (we say performance), and better staff engagement. And so much less internal drama.

Why bigger? Bigger is all about boosting performance (quality output) to create predictable profitability. By investing in training on how to think and solve problems differently (we say genius thinking) our most successful clients differentiated themselves in the marketplace. Because they had built their infrastructure to support rapid growth (be better) they were able to absorb the growth and attract better staff and customers.

Why bolder? Bolder is all about being able to fulfill on a big vision (your why). It means the infrastructure (better and bigger) is designed to support the kind of growth most owners wish they had. Our clients say when they have this kind of alignment their job becomes fun. Their staff are more satisfied. Their clients love them.

In her practice as a value-added reseller (VAR) of accounting software, coauthor Rosemary fell prey to all the blunders when she hit Transition. She was the smartest one in her office. She was the most creative and most strategic. And she was the best troubleshooter in the business. She loved the role – it made her feel important and valued because she was involved in every decision. Yet the company's growth and profitability started to stall out. Adding more sales was not helping.

A pretty big shift in thinking was needed.

She saw, by focusing on a culture of excellence (leadership element) and performance (profitability element), she could train her staff to identify and solve the right (or root) problem. Then, to level up her project managers' thinking, Rosemary involved them in designing genius client solutions. Two things happened: More prospects closed, and profit increased (better staff performance). The result was the organization tripled in size within eighteen months.

As the general manager of a large printing plant, coauthor Bob kept focusing on productivity, how the team could be more efficient by running the presses faster or changing between the jobs quicker. And the team became more and more demoralized.

A change in thinking was needed.

Bob began to wonder if meeting production goals wasn't about leadership pounding the table harder to get people to hear them—maybe it was about redefining the problem and the solution.

When Bob asked the team to focus on performance (better quality output) they identified some maintenance issues that were causing the presses to run slower. They proposed a genius solution by redesigning the workspace. That solved two things. First, they restaged the tools, parts, and raw materials so less time was wasted looking for things. That led to a new design of maintenance procedures. This shift in thinking opened the capacity for an additional $1.5 million in revenue and happier, more engaged associates.

Key Takeaways:

1. Transition is a phase between emerging lifecycle stage and professionally managed lifecycle stage. It causes a barrier to growth.

2. Breaking the Transition barrier happens when a company's internal systems support the external market buy-in.

3. The Predictable Profitability System allows a CEO to strategically focus on the whole company—big picture.

4. Change your thinking, change your results.

PART II

THE PATHWAY TO A BETTER, BIGGER BUSINESS

3

UNDERSTAND
THE FUNDAMENTAL PROBLEM

*"If you think as a leader you can and should solve all the
problems, then you're both wrong and significantly constrain-
ing the capacity of the organization to be creative."*
Tim Brown, CEO, IDEO

Most of us believe the job of a CEO or leader of a business
line is simple: keep your people producing at maximum
efficiency. Many leaders think the best way to do that is to be
the master problem solver.

Take Joe for example. He runs a $36 million company, and
he spends all day fielding questions. He is exhausted because
he had fallen prey to blunder three (managing the urgent over
the important) and blunder four (having the entire company
rely on his expertise to solve problems). Worse, the company's
growth has stalled out, even as he puts in more and more hours
solving problems.

When Joe asked us to help grow his revenue, we suggested
instead that he might want to start with solving blunder four.

He quickly saw that by answering all the questions his staff posed he had become a crutch and a roadblock. He also saw, by not asking them to offer solutions, his staff had stopped thinking and started waiting for answers. Joe saw the company was limited because only he was solving problems. By training and empowering his staff to resolve issues like he did, he got better decisions. Better results. All of which translated into increased growth for the firm.

To re-engage his staff's thinking, Joe posted a sign at his front door: Don't bring a problem without at least two solutions. His job got easier—the funny thing is his staff thought he got a lot smarter overnight. Empowering his staff to handle things on the front lines without involving all of the chain of command to confirm solutions, created efficiencies which translated into profit. When Joe got out of the way, eliminating blunders three and four, the whole team engaged in new ways to solve problems (genius thinking). In eight years, the company has tripled in size and Joe has gone from a seventy-five-hour workweek to something less than forty hours per week.

Becoming Better By Solving The Right Problem

To eradicate blunder four, a CEO must move beyond the fundamental problem of thinking "my role, as the leader, is to drive productivity" (which requires you to be at the epicenter of every key decision). The right problem to solve is "how to train the staff to identify the right problem." While that may seem straightforward, we have found that there is an inherent difficulty called "confirmation bias" that mucks things up quickly. Confirmation bias embeds your solution as the problem rather than driving for the root issue. Joe solved that by posting the sign "bring two solutions" ending his Groundhog Day dilemma of being the master problem solver.

The Problem Is The Problem

Because we know how good CEOs are at problem solving, we thought it might be a fun experiment to ask what they thought are the top three problems emerging firms experience. Then we wanted to find out how they thought those issues ought to be resolved. We noticed something fascinating, not in *what* was identified but *how* they identified them. In rank order these emerging firm CEOs said their top three issues are:

1. They need more revenue because they don't have enough money to do what is needed for the business to grow (blunder one).

2. They need to find a unicorn (a diamond in the rough they can mold) because they cannot afford the best people—bigger companies are luring them away (blunder two).

3. They need more time in the day to solve all the urgent problems that need solutions (blunder three).

Notice that the problem named, more revenue, a unicorn, and more time is a conclusion of the actual problem: they didn't have the profits needed to reinvest in the company. When we asked them how they tried to solve these problems, they said:

1. They sought counsel from:
   a. Peers/Other CEOs (the successful ones who had broken the $10 million growth barrier) on how to grow sales or find unicorns

    b. Books and articles on how to grow sales

    c. YouTube videos on how to grow the business

2. They hired a marketing or sales consultant to help them grow sales

3. They hired a "hunter" salesperson to grow sales

Consider that they were seeking solutions to their bias, and not the actual problem first identified. That is confirmation bias in action. Their solutions were skewed to their embedded solution, and not the actual, root issue. This can be an expensive detour. In this case, emerging CEOs thought driving for more sales would solve all their problems.

We then asked CEOs, who already have mastered their first Transition (broke through the $10 million sales barrier) and are in peer groups like Vistage, The Alternative Board, or Renaissance Forum, what they thought the problem and solution was for the emerging CEO. These professionally managed CEOs most often say it is "an organizational infrastructure" problem. The problem they were trying to solve, or thought the emerging CEOs needed to solve, was greater profitability. And these CEOs know that if they implement standard operating procedures (SOPs) it will drive the kinds of efficiencies that ensure profitability. In plain English they are saying: to drive performance give the staff detailed instructions[9] on how to do their jobs so they can be as efficient as possible.

They give this advice because they know at the professionally managed stage of a business (which is where they are) their growth element and their leadership element have been defined and are working. They have aligned their team to fulfill the company objectives and fine-tuned standard operating procedures across all activities, thus ensuring staff engagement and profitability. Unfortunately, emerging stage firms often have an ill-defined leadership element, and a profit element that is insufficient to sustain the advancement of their company. So when they focus on production it can lead to staff burnout or departure.

In short, just driving for efficiency when in Transition often causes more trouble than it solves.

The second piece of advice they give focuses on culture. Many of the books and articles they encourage reading focus on culture. Like Simon Sinek's book *Start with Why*[10]—he says that having a well-defined purpose and culture will help your staff make better decisions. Various Harvard Business Review articles on culture talk about how defining your culture provides the environment for staff to want to work harder and make better decisions. Their objective in encouraging culture is to help create engaged, motivated staff who know how to make better business decisions for you. And the professionally managed CEOs know that once you have your SOPs in place, culture promotes engaged staff who then drive the result you desire efficiently and effectively. Another way of saying this is: if your culture and your defined way of making decisions aligns to your leadership element, it will drive the performance of your staff.

Unfortunately, many leaders when first facing Transition think enhancing culture is about perks rather than a clearly defined method of decision-making. Without that, staff tend to be more inefficient and less profitable.

A third recommendation professionally managed stage CEOs make is to focus on metrics. As they say, "the thing measured is the thing done". Because CEOs of large companies cannot be involved in every aspect and every decision, they have to rely on trends to let them know where to focus. Metrics are designed to help executives focus on and get done what matters most—staying focused on the right stuff. The problem here is finding the right metrics, and particularly the right key performance metrics, is a time intensive pursuit (at least six months). Rarely is it the first place to start. Consider doing this second.

While all of these solutions are valid, and at some point they will need to be implemented for continuous growth to occur, it is vital to know where you should start based on your company particulars.

Meet Mark

Mark's company earns $6 million in revenue and $1.2 million in net profit. By all accounts, a successful company although his growth is becoming unpredictable and inconsistent. Mark wants better. Being in Transition he knows he has to do three things:

1. Identify his root problem(s).
2. Review his business framework for leaks in performance.
3. Determine what in his foundation needs to change so his company can grow 10X without breaking.

He started with his framework to identify gaps in performance. His foundation element (how he delivers product and attracts customers) could not accommodate the growth he wanted. In its current design it could only produce more by adding headcount. This is root problem number one.

His growth element (how he makes money) would not allow for the expanded growth and the increased profitability he ultimately wants without a lot of investment in time, money, and effort. Root problem number two is that his overhead costs are in lockstep with revenue.

His leadership and profit elements were not identifying and solving the root problems. The staff were at capacity. Everyone was in production mode—and becoming inefficient. Root problem number three.

Once he had detected the glitches in his framework and named the root problems, he was ready to engage the team in genius thinking.

He started by asking how he could increase efficiencies without adding overhead? His team suggested adding new software that provided a better interface for his clients and greater efficiencies for his staff.

Next, how could he get his leadership team to think differently? They needed to define a strategic lens that would identify which problems to work on first, second, third. First, he hired an operations manager (whom he taught to make decisions like he did). Then he had her train the staff to think the same way.

Then, how could he change the staff from a pure productivity mindset (quantity of output) to a performance mindset (quality of output)? Together they redefined their metrics to be performance driven.

Mark's results? Two year later, his company is in the same building, with the same number of production staff and earning $60 million in revenue and $24 million in profits. Mark used the Predictable Profitability System to help him uncover his root problems and determine where to start.

The Predictable Profitability System Will Guide You

The Predictable Profitability System provides a methodology by which to manage your business issues more effectively. Knowing where to start matters in Transition, where the most common trait is a lack of resources.

Most executives start with refining business processes when profitability or cash flow become an issue because they know that their foundation must support growth—and before Transition that worked. But now, concentrating only on the *foundation-growth line* forces the executive to become the chief problem solver (blunder four). That substantially slows growth.

Our clients found they got better results when they focused instead on *the leadership-profit relationship*. To develop leadership within their organizations they started with defining a company strategic lens that described how decisions are made in their company. This strategic lens helps staff to be much more successful at uncovering the root issues. That clarity and alignment opens the door to genius thinking and maximizing growth.

Using The System

If you are creating a company from scratch the order in which most leaders define their framework is: growth, foundation, leadership, profitability. Transition forces a company to revisit and redefine how it produces revenue and turn it into the growth element. However, we do not recommend starting there based on what our clients have reported to us.

Our clients say it works best to re-engage the staff first. They like to start with defining culture, the leadership element, then assessing performance, the profit element. Once they have been fine-tuned, they move to the growth element to engage genius thinking.

Once all that is in place the foundation can be tweaked to accommodate the cumulative changes.

This Isn't Kansas, Dorothy

We have looked at the importance of defining the problem correctly and finding the root issue. We have introduced the Predictable Profitability System as a new way of thinking about how your company is put together. And we have shared how Transition messes with what should be straight forward resolutions to your issues.

A good analogy about Transition is: Just as puberty is a normal phase in everyone's maturation there just isn't anything normal about this time. The behaviors and strategies parents use to resolve issues in this phase are anything but straight forward and easy. Ask any parent. It is like all the rules just flew out the window and none of the strategies that used to work do anymore. Doing more of the same and expecting different results is the very definition of insanity. Try something new.

New Thinking: A Quick Guide To Determine The Root Problem

1. Inconsistent or unpredictable revenue:

   Analyze market buy-in. Find out what the market is really buying from you.

   Review your growth element. Check how you deliver your product/service. Is it effective and efficient? Is it antiquated? Does it produce the sales you want?

2. Diminishing productivity:

   Check your growth element – see #1 above. Does it need to change?

   Next review your leadership element. Are decisions made in support of greater performance?

   Test your metrics for alignment to culture, growth element and performance mindset.

3. High staff turnover:

Refine your leadership element. Your existing culture indicates there is some kind of inconsistency between the values of the firm and the behaviors that are rewarded.

Next refine your growth element. If it focuses only on productivity, you may be invoking turnover.

4. Trouble finding the right staff:

Refine your leadership element, specifically the company's why and values. Talk about that in interviews.

Key Takeaways:

1. Figure out the right problem to solve. Avoid confirmation bias when defining the problem.

2. Transition changes the answers to the problems.

3. Use the Predictable Profitability System as your strategic lens to know where to start.

4. Managing blunder three (managing the urgent) is exhausting. Stop it.

5. Determine what is yours alone as CEO to do and delegate the rest.

4
FIX YOUR REVENUE WOES

*"… if I had more revenue I could solve all
my business issues…"*

Meet Beth

Beth owns an IT firm that is in Transition and she wants to grow. We were meeting to discuss a particular problem that has been keeping her up at night. For twenty minutes she poured out her frustration and her deep concerns. She is worried about losing key staff. The IT industry is hot, and it is getting harder to find enough good people to hire, much less preventing her best people from getting poached. She is starting to have trouble affording new technicians. On top of all that, some key staff are in jeopardy of leaving because of infighting. She summarized her problem as: the talent pool is too small to find and pay for the caliber of staff needed because the bigger firms are offering higher salaries than she can afford (blunder two – finding a unicorn).

We decided to try an experiment. We asked her: if we could find a consultant to solve your staffing problems—that thing she stated was keeping her up at night—or a consultant who will help you increase revenue who would you pick?

Without skipping a beat, she said she would hire the sales consultant to increase revenue (blunder one). Why? She thinks if she has more money she could attract the kind of talent she wants and she could give valued staff raises and stay competitive with the market. In her mind she restated the staffing issue, as a revenue problem. She thinks increasing sales will solve that. She has collapsed her solution into how she defined the problem before she even looked at how to determine or solve the root problem.

Adding Revenue Is the Wrong Solution To The Wrong Problem

Like Beth, many CEOs think if they just sell more, it will solve everything. They could then hire better staff. They would have enough time to focus on the strategic issues. They would have enough money to fix the infrastructure issues they have.

Typical Growth Model

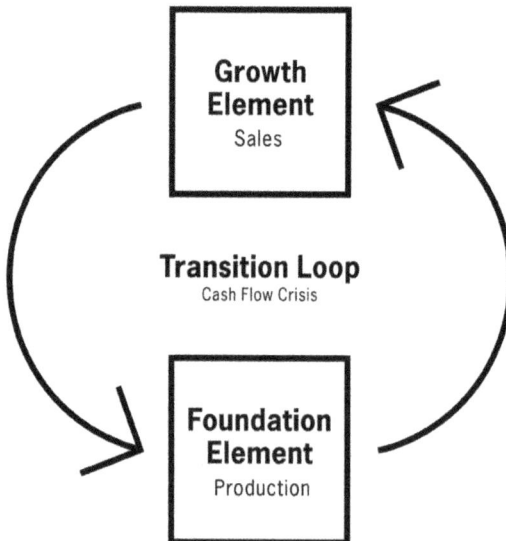

```
                Growth
                Element
                 Sales

              Transition Loop
              Cash Flow Crisis

              Foundation
               Element
              Production
```

This focus or need for more revenue when there is not enough money in the business is a twofold problem for emerging leaders. First, they believe sales is equated to growth. CEOs in the professionally managed stage understand that is not so. They are looking for market share (which means they want more market buy-in) not just more revenue. And second, emerging leaders think that adding sales is the solution to the cash flow problem they are experiencing because they think it will put more money in the bank.

There are better ways to solve cash flow problems than just adding more customers. Adding sales may seem like the fastest solution. It isn't. Instead, when there is a cash flow problem, focus first on making the business profitable. Then focus on growth.

Blunder one (sales is the cure-all) came into being after we saw time and time again the honest but misguided thinking that many consultants and CEOs use to deal with cash flow and other money issues owners have at this stage in a business's lifecycle.

Thinking any sale is a good sale enhances your business risk without benefit. When margins (the gross profit per job) are squeezed, making a mistake or being inefficient on the job, can erode profits and put your company in jeopardy. Saying yes to any sale is not a good idea.

Meet Randy

Randy, an emerging CEO, was saying yes to every sale and a fair amount of it was marginally profitable. Low profits added onto higher overhead spell trouble. For Randy it meant he was running out of money. That had him falling prey to blunder three (managing the urgent) on top of blunder one (sales as a cure-all).

Randy wants the quickest way out of this mess.

To accomplish this, he re-examined his growth element to find what they were best at. What he saw was too much of staff time was spent supporting marginal sales and not enough time on their sweet spot (what they were best at). By changing the company's focus to sell and support only the service they were best equipped to deliver, staff performance increased. They were more engaged and produced a higher quality product.

The team went on to deliver big results. They are now growing an average of 44 percent year over year for eight years running. They doubled net profit in the first year (from 5 percent to 10 percent) and doubled it again the next year to 20 percent. That is called predictable profitability.

Randy's company got better when they identified and solved the right problem.

Adding more projects to an already inefficient process, like Randy's or Beth's, will only add to the frustration of the entire staff. Pressing them to doing more work in less time has them sacrifice even more quality which lowers profitability even more. Adding sales does not solve this problem.

Competitively pricing your product/service to 'buy' market share is the same as buying marginal sales. You end up attracting more of the price conscious customers, not your ideal customer. Many inexperienced leaders fall into this trap because they are so focused on adding revenue. They end up increasing their risk of doing business and not solving their cash flow issue.

Can you see then that adding any sales in Transition (especially spending money on marketing to attract clients) might not be the right answer? And that "not all sales are created equally"? For a company in Transition it is miscalculated thinking because the root problem has yet to be uncovered.

The Right Problem To Solve

The time has come to make a new decision based on new information. The right problem to solve (when you need money) is how to become profitable. There are two components to this notion. First is to shift from a production to a performance mindset. Second is to find that thing only your firm can do that the market *must* have (we call that your scalability factor or "S-factor").

A performance mindset requires that the foundation is functional, meaning the organization can deliver its product/service efficiently (more) and effectively (higher quality). Without this in place adding sales will implode a company.

Being profitable is a strong measure of the market's buy-in[11] to your ideas, your product, your service, and it will help show you which product or service to scale.

How Qualcomm Found The Key To Scale

Coauthor Rosemary had the opportunity to hear the founder of Qualcomm, Irwin Jacobs, speak several years ago. He shared how finding his S-factor reset Qualcomm.

Some background: Jacobs and Andrew Viterbi cofounded Qualcomm in 1985. In 1992, its main business was put on a government hold forcing the company into Transition because their existing revenue model broke. They needed to scale so they started looking for what they could do that others could not. They settled on CDMA. Today Qualcomm is a billion-dollar firm in the telecom industry founded on CDMA, a product they could scale, and it looks nothing like their original revenue model.

Time and time again business founders say their business today looks nothing like what they thought when they started out. Successful CEOs say when they faced a Transition moment, they had to rethink their revenue model and turn it into a growth element. They had to learn how to be better, bigger and bolder. And that takes a new way of thinking.

Meet John

When John's company reached $3 million in revenue, he added a second salesperson to begin scaling but profitability did not follow suit. John was stuck.

As John saw it, the only way to achieve better profitability was to raise prices[12] even though sales teams rarely think raising prices is a good idea. Because John works with Fortune 500 companies, he knows they will not take kindly to price increases without a good reason or without added services.

John's company is in Transition (revenue size), so he knows he needs to start by asking himself a few questions. They are:

- Were his sales "good" sales or marginal sales?

- What were his customers really buying (buy-in)?
- Was he profitable enough to scale?
- Was there another service he could offer (leading to his S-factor)?

John discovered he was not profitable enough yet to scale. In doing a deep dive into his scalability element he found not all his customers were created equally from a profit perspective. He also noticed that his best clients bought their services in a bundle.

John decided to focus the company only on the most profitable sales that his best customers wanted. He started by asking his customers what they really wanted. By asking them without his confirmation bias interfering with the process, John got unexpected and fruitful answers. This allowed him to streamline his offerings that fit what the market really wanted. He had uncovered his S-factor.

Sales and profits went up because he could charge more and do less to retain his best clients while attracting more of the same.

Results: Having a bundled product allowed the sales team to grow existing client accounts as well as attract new markets. Overall sales started growing at a 30 percent clip year over year. Coupled with a production team now focused on delivering the type of service in their wheelhouse, they could focus on performance which caused a 50 percent increase (not a typo) in profitability. Best yet, he worked more with his ideal clients.

By focusing first on better profitability, John saw he needed to change how he delivered his service (growth-foundation relationship). Then he fine-tuned the internal team's performance. Better performance had the market wanting more (buy-in). And that drove sustainable growth and profitability (leadership-profit relationship). John was now ready to scale.

Buy-in: Your External Key To Uncovering Your S-Factor

Market buy-in creates a pull for what you are selling and how you deliver your services, drawing in more sales which helps add to the bottom line. Most business owners assume incorrectly that they know why their customers are buying from them. When you know why the customer is buying from you, identifying your S-factor becomes easier.

Unless and until we actually know why our customers buy from us[13] we are likely to waste our marketing budget and be frustrated that we are not growing as quickly as we would like or think we can. Do not assume you know. Ask your client. You may be surprised what they are really buying from you.

Meet Michael

Michael thought he knew what his customers were buying. When he followed Jaynie Smith's[14] guidelines to use a market focus group, he found something very different. It was not the price he was charging that his clients were buying, rather it was the ease in locating where they were in Michael's product delivery cycle that made all the difference. They were buying transparency and convenience. His firm provided an easy portal to find out where the product was in its cycle of delivery. And what, if anything, was holding it up so that it could be resolved faster. What are your clients really buying from you? Find out so you can more wisely spend your marketing money to attract the right client.

More importantly, check every few years to see if the answer remains the same or the customers want something new.

Transition causes added complexity in how you deliver your product or service. It muddies the waters around finding, naming and therefore solving the core issues in a business. All of which make it harder to uncover your S-factor.

While it represents a big opportunity it also potentially creates a big risk for a business. There is something in your growth element that must come to an end. Something new is wanting to emerge to continue the company's growth and development. It can be a destructive or a creative cycle, depending upon your perspective and approach. And the regular rules of business no longer apply. Adding sales is not the answer. Becoming profitable and defining leadership comes first. Then adding sales will work.

Note:
We are often asked if just adding revenue is ever the answer. In two instances the answer is yes. The first place is when you are just starting out and may not yet know your market sweet spot. Hint: if you are at or above $1 million in revenue, you have passed this point.

And the second time is when you are in the professionally managed stage and already have a sound foundational element and an effective leadership element (check your profit line for verification). You will naturally add *profitable* sales as a result.

Focus on driving sales only when your profitability is already sufficient to carry the company. A good rule of thumb is at least 15 percent net profitability.

Key Takeaways:

1. Manage your cash flow by becoming profitable. Then grow.
2. Become profitable by focusing on sales that are in your wheelhouse.
3. Create buy-in, internally and externally, to ignite scaling.
4. Find your scalability factor by finding out what your clients are really buying (a focus group study is a great way to do that).

5
FIND THE RIGHT PEOPLE

"I have so many opportunities to grow the business to the next level, if only I could find better staff or get my existing staff to be more productive."

The second biggest problem leaders tell us they have relates to staff. It runs the gamut from not being able to find the right person for the job to hiring a junior level person hoping they can ramp up quickly. It includes not hiring the experienced person soon enough to not firing poor performers quickly enough. Often the business climate makes it even tougher to hire top tier staff.

In an ideal world you want clear communication between your staff with less (preferably no) office drama. You want the most productive output with the least expense (some companies push work down to the least paid person hoping for cheaper overall output). And you want your staff to produce their work with the highest quality, in the manner originally designed, quickly and efficiently. You want your organization to be better.

When we interviewed CEOs, they characterized much of their staff as good but not great. They defined many of their staff as "C players", doing the bare minimum. Enough to not get fired but not enough to help the team move to the next level. They said they had mostly marginal contributors who were not very coachable and somewhat unmotivated or disengaged. And they described these C players as staff who tend to blame others for their lack of performance (their peers, their boss are the problem, not them). If you have even one person on your team that fits this description you are jeopardizing the performance of the entire team—and affecting your bottom line.

Everyone else has to compensate and that lowers their game. A 2022 Gallup Poll found nearly 70 percent of staff are disengaged. How can an organization grow if seventy percent of staff are disengaged?

Most CEOs we talk to are frustrated beyond measure at this point because they really do want engaged, intelligent employees and find they are just making do. They wonder why their staff are not more engaged or seem to behave more like mindless workers than the talented folks they first hired. One of our clients asked us, why are my people checking their minds at the door?

Did you really do such a bad job during the hiring phase that you ended up with so many mediocre players? Is it really impossible to find qualified staff at a salary you can afford? Maybe the problem is not finding good staff, maybe the problem is something else.

The Problem Is Not Finding The Unicorn

It is a trap thinking a unicorn is the solution because who you really want is unavailable at the salary and benefits you can afford. Like Oakland A's general manager Billy Beane said in the movie *Moneyball*, "The problem we're trying to solve is that there are rich teams and there are poor teams...and then there's us. It's an unfair game. We've got to think differently."

Here is how some of our clients first looked at their staffing problem:

Marielle: She cannot find good staff accountants who want to work in public accounting. She says the problem is the pool of candidates is drying up. Fewer young people are getting degrees in accounting.

Harvey: He cannot find young attorneys willing to put in 2500 hours per year (averaging more than 50 hours per week). His business model is that they should "pay their dues" over three to four years because it cannot support hiring more people.

Ian: He cannot find skilled labor willing to work minimum wage doing construction on ships because the housing industry is paying a lot more for the same skill.

Can you hear they are trying to find a unicorn, the exception to the conclusions they have drawn in their marketplace? The problem *really* is they have an antiquated revenue model (part of their scalable growth element) that drives productivity rather than seeks performance. The reality is that fewer people want to "prove themselves" by working long hours.

The Real Problem Is A Leadership Mindset Issue

When an owner pushes productivity in Transition, it causes three problems—the first is decreased profitability, the second is the loss of high performers, and the third is not being able to find and hire talent.

So consider the problem is not how to find a unicorn who will work for next to nothing that you can train into a top producer. Consider the real problem is: how to turn existing staff into high performers.

A new leadership mindset is needed that is centered on bringing out the best in staff. That requires a shift from a productivity mindset to a performance mindset. And it means creating programs that train and engage staff in thinking and decision-making.

From Productivity To Performance

Business leaders with cashflow problems and staff retention issues tend to get stuck in a productivity mindset. To increase cashflow they think getting staff to produce more is the answer. It is not. It's like when your tire gets stuck in a rut. Hitting the gas pedal (increasing productivity of the tire) does nothing to remove the tire from the hole. It does though, spread mud or grit (unhappy staff). Something else is needed to extract oneself. Consider a shift in focus from quantity of yield (production) to quality of yield (performance). Changing the focus from "what we do" to "how we do it" helps engage staff and that is the first step in creating predictable profitability.

What Your Employees Really Want

When hiring, the best candidates are looking for something besides the highest pay. Yes, they want perks and benefits. And they want to be rewarded for performance. Career and leadership growth opportunities trump the ping pong table and snacks all day long. Flexibility around work times and remote work are increasingly important. What they want is leadership opportunities and training and they want to be inspired by the leaders they work for.

A new way to think about this is to ask yourself if you have a clear picture of what candidates are buying when they accept your position. In the old days, people took jobs to advance their careers or to provide steady income or to have a pension at the end. These days people are looking for companies that are positively impacting society or providing novel products or are an exciting place to work. Be prepared that the most talented folks out there can and will ask for much more than just salary[15].

Meet Rose

Rose is an excellent accountant. She was happy in her job when she got a call from a headhunter who knows her caliber (the best candidates are rarely looking for work). The headhunter said, "the company is excellent but is paying 20 percent less than what you are currently making." She let the headhunter know that there is only one company that she would consider taking a 20 percent pay cut for. Turns out it is this company. Rose took the job on the condition that the company give her a 20 percent raise at the end of the first year. She was willing to prove herself to work at the company of her dreams. She had heard great things about the CEO and the culture. The best team had been assembled at this company. Rose wanted to learn leadership from them and experience being on the best team. She also enjoyed the flexibility the company afforded her as her family grew. Four years later she says it was well worth the move.

Create The Opportunity For Staff To Become Engaged

Your objective with each new hire is to create staff engagement from the first moment you speak with them. When they see an opportunity for personal growth it invites their engagement.

Starting with the interviewing process be clear about the big future that you have for your firm. Paint a very bright outlook for the firm. A caution here though, do not oversell where you are. Make sure you let them know exactly when you intend to get there. Five years out, one year out. Be clear and honest about what is in the way. If they are the right fit, that gap will not scare them away. It will, instead, attract them to your company because they want to be part of making history with you. It also helps them to stay when some unexpected bumps in the road occur.

Then talk about how you will develop them once they are hired. Consider a leadership plan (aka a succession plan) that outlines how you intend to develop the staff's leadership capacities that matches a staff's talents with a career path.

The interview process creates buy-in. Your leadership element turns buy-in into engagement and loyalty.

Leadership Tools To Develop Staff

As a leader, you recognize that your people are your most valuable asset. Consistency in words, actions, praise and corrective actions with all staff allows them to understand that. Your leadership element should be designed to build trust and a strong platform upon which to be engaged.

It does that by providing staff with a roadmap on how to make decisions, what behaviors are important to the company (and which are not), and what will be measured. We like to call that your strategic lens.

A well-defined strategic lens helps staff to identify root issues, then name them without confirmation bias. When a person understands the objective (why), what is important to the company (metrics) and what behaviors will be tolerated (culture) it is easy to stay focused and feel valued. It eliminates waste and distractions in a company by creating clarity, alignment and staff engagement.

There are three components to the strategic lens:

1. *Purpose Driver – The Why*

This defines the reason a company is in business and what kind of future the CEO intends to create. It helps develop clarity and unambiguity about *what* it is doing, *where* it is going and *why* all that matters. It also helps prevent the shiny ball syndrome, or side excursions, that do not serve the business. This is a filter by which all decisions can be made. As Charles, one of our clients, tells his staff, "If you want a project funded in the company, tell me how it fulfills our purpose, and your project will be financed."

2. Culture Driver – The Performance Filter

Culture is all about the mores of conduct and decision-making in a company. It uses the values of a company to encourage desired behaviors and discourage undesired behaviors. The point of culture is to encourage actions that support the leader's goals. As James, one of our clients likes to say, "My culture tells me how much the team respects my leadership."

3. Metrics Driver – The Measures

Metrics, by design, measure alignment to goals, identify the gaps, and provide an objective scorecard of the company's progress. The point of metrics is to reduce assumptions, identify any misalignments or faulty data interpretation. It allows staff and management to drive clarity on what and how the company executes. As Susie, a client of ours likes to say, "I live and manage by my metrics dashboard. It lets me quickly hone in on potential issues."

Meet Jean

Jean is struggling in her job because management is giving mixed instructions on how she is to report progress on assignments. Her production is slowing down as she spends more time figuring out the 'right way' to document her work and analyze problems. Now, her realization (billed time versus budgeted time) is dropping, and the company is blaming her.

This company's leadership element (how she is to perform) affected Jean's ability to execute. Plus, the company did not agree about the mission critical processes (foundation). Were they documented? You bet. Ultimately, the company lost Jean who had been a high performer because management inconsistently executed its processes.

A high performer consistently produces results above the company's norms. High performance, without staff engagement, is unsustainable. Burnout happens. Staff engagement is defined as the intersection of an employee's full contribution to fulfilling the company's purpose plus their total job satisfaction. This intersection creates a sustainable, high level of performance. Staff are aligned to the firm's overarching goals, direction, and purpose. They believe their job not only fulfills those objectives but also fulfills their own personal objectives. Everyone is happy.

A Caveat

If you hear someone is leaving due to "compensation" please know that is rarely the real reason—even though it ranks in the top three reasons. It is the most expedient, least offensive thing to say. The more likely reason they are leaving is due to the culture and or the boss. That is a difficult topic to discuss when a person is working in the company, and not worth the effort to discuss when they are leaving.

Key Takeaways:

1. Use the three components of a strategic lens to drive staff engagement.
2. Create a plan that defines how you will support your staff's growth.

3. Have a clearly defined on-boarding process. Remember turnover begins with a misaligned recruiting and on-boarding process.

4. Do not create or settle for C players. Train staff into A players.

5. Surprise, you may already have the right people and all you really need to do is develop them.

6
CREATE MORE TIME

"I need a twenty-six-hour day."

We hear that from CEOs all the time.

Resonate with you? The one finite resource we all must deal with is time. More money can be generated. People can be replaced. Work or office space can be added. Time, however, once it is gone, it is gone. It is something we all face and it can cause a leader to do the expedient thing, not necessarily the best thing.

The problem CEOs say they have is that there simply is not enough time to solve all the internal staff problems that are coming at them and figure out the company's three-to-five-year plan much less manage whatever the economy is throwing at them. Definitely exhausting if one lives with:

> "There is never enough time to do it right, but there is always enough time to do it over."

> Or, the corollary

"If there isn't enough time to do it right the first time, where will you find the time to fix it and do it over?"[16]

The Problem Isn't There Is Not Enough Time

Often CEOs feel like they are playing a daily game of whack-a-mole, handling the urgent, but not necessarily important, problems each day. Consequently, too much time is spent working *in* the business, dealing with the nuts and bolts, rather than working *on* the business (reinforcing culture, driving strategy, and building relationships in fulfillment of its why). This is the essence of blunder three: managing the urgent over the important. It also reflects blunder four—overreliance on the CEO's talent since many of these problems could and should be handled by others in the organization. But the CEO becomes the chief problem solver because the company's decision-making process has not been documented or shared, leaving the CEO unable to delegate to others.

Time and again we've found that CEOs of companies facing Transition mistake "busyness" for being productive, effective, and valuable. And they think the only way to break Transition's growth barrier is to be involved in every decision. It is a way of ensuring that they are needed and essential. However, in our research, we have found that sometimes CEOs use "busy" to hide feeling like an "imposter", not wanting to admit that they don't really know what the CEO role is. The Transition CEO's job is to define the company's strategic lens, so that the staff can be effective and follow a successful leader.

Can you see the problem isn't that you need more time but is that you are not doing your job? You're doing someone else's job.

Meet Ryan

When Ryan started his own marketing firm, he was an expert in one of the products they conducted market research on so he put himself in charge of that business line. Several years into running his firm, he was still doing that production work, causing him to be a part-time CEO at best. Ryan recognized that to be a full-time CEO he needed to hire someone to take over that production work. It took him a little over a year to let go. And then we got the call. Ryan asked, "What am I supposed to do now?"

The job of a CEO has two components, an internal and external focus. Internally, it is to influence staff thinking and increase market value. To do that, a CEO sets the strategy of the company and provides the resources (time, money, staff, infrastructure) needed to execute that strategy. By defining and enforcing the culture of the firm a CEO assures alignment to his or her strategic lens.

Externally, the CEO is the link between the marketplace and the firm. And again, it is to influence market thinking and increase market share. None of which can be measured day-to-day, only over time.

Malcolm Gladwell, in his book *Outlier*[17] says it takes 10,000 hours to master a craft. At fifty hours per week, that equates to a little over four work years in the CEO seat. From interviewing CEOs, consultants and other professionals over the years, this notion seems right. While a leader might have the title or role, it takes three to five years to figure out and feel comfortable doing the CEO job. It seems, then, that the reason why CEOs continue to be subjected to whack-a-mole might be the CEO.

Meet Paul And Adam

Adam, a CEO of a $30 million company, was having trouble scaling. He asked Paul, a CEO of a $60 million company to advise him. Paul started by asking him about the projects Adam was specifically working on in terms of when they would come to fruition. No project had a life of greater than nine months (meaning that a project would go from ideation to completion in a maximum of nine months). Paul explained that a CEO needs to be thinking at least two to three years out otherwise the "important" gets swept away by the urgent. Any short-term projects (less than a year to execute) belong to the COO or Operations Manager, he explained. Adam realized that he couldn't scale because all his time was taken up doing the COOs job, not his own. And yes, Adam did have a COO.

The sad truth is that the growth of any firm is dependent upon how many problems a CEO can handle in a day. At some point, the CEO will become overwhelmed with all the things they have to do and wind up becoming ineffective in the quest for a twenty-six-hour day.

Consider this: if there are not enough people to delegate to or the staff does not have the skillset to be delegated to, it is a planning and training problem. Is there a plan to determine the right timing to add and train new staff? Or is there a profit problem and the growth element needs an overhaul? If the CEO spends too much time dealing with the urgent (we call that working *in* the business) and not enough time on what's important (we call that working *on* the business) things like resource management fall to the wayside. The business becomes stuck.

The result is the CEO winds up putting a governor on the business. This may cause the company to lose out on the revenue or profit required to fuel the momentum needed to break the barrier. A CEO who tries to be the chief problem solver becomes the most expensive staffer in the company while leaving the organization without what it really needs, a leader.

The Right Problem Is: What Is The CEO's Role?

Most often CEOs in Transition (like Ryan) ask, what is the CEO's role, anyway? We find that there are two types of CEOs: A conductor and an operations manager. The conductor is a bridge between the external world and the staff that run the day-to-day business. The conductor role unifies the team, sets the tempo, shapes the business's strategy, and relays that vision to all the performers much like an orchestra conductor. The CEO sets the goal, and the staff deliver. This structure allows for scaling a company.

The other role, operations manager, runs the internal business, overseeing the planning, organizing, and supervising of the firm's production. They create the efficiencies needed to be profitable. They make sure it all gets done. This structure is designed to maintain status quo for a company because it is all about today and not planning for tomorrow.

Which are you: the conductor or the operations manager? Find out by looking at where you spend *most* of your time—the left or right side of the columns below. Hint: when in Transition you will straddle the fence between the two until you resolve blunders three and four.

CEO As Conductor Guides The Business	CEO As Operations Manager Runs The Business
Develops future strategic alliances (time span three to five years)	Manages today's problems (time span less than one year)
Designs how an organization delivers	Manages what the organization delivers
Allocates resources to projects	Manages the resources on a project
Increases the value of the business	Increases the efficiency of the business
Builds a strategic lens	Is the chief problem solver
Develops the purpose	Drives the results (KPI s)

Doing both, among other things, was possible when your business was "mom and pop". Now that your business has grown, you want others to run the day-to-day, leaving you to guide the business. If your destination is to break the $10 million barrier, how can you expect to do that without having a strategy and the right kind of managers to execute that strategy?

> "The greatest leader is not necessarily the one who does the greatest things. He is the one who gets others to do the greatest things."[18]
>
> Ronald Reagan

If you, as CEO, continue to do everything yourself, your people will never reach their full potential and give their best effort to your business. Nor will you. You will end up with a bunch of C players on your team making your company less fun and harder to run.

You may have heard the adage that we teach people how we want to be treated. This means that, as the CEO, if you continue to do the things that others could (or should) do themselves, guess what, they are never going to take initiative. Or if you criticize any attempt they make to be proactive, they will stop making decisions and just ask you. It's much easier than being reprimanded or made to feel stupid. Treat them like they cannot make good decisions and they will not make any decisions (learned helplessness).

Your job is to train others to think.

At some point, the CEO needs to focus on new horizons for the company. If the organization has a good foundation, a clearly defined way of making money, alignment of leadership and effective staff at all levels[19], there is no reason why every issue has to bubble up to the CEO. The people accountable for a particular function will know which problems are theirs to solve and which belong to the CEO. Maybe it is time to look at how to restructure the CEO role and become a conductor.

CEO Role Newly Defined

As an emerging business leader you are involved in the day-to-day decisions and operations of the business. And yet, to continue growing it is important to delegate and start thinking strategically. That means your perspective must shift from being internally to externally focused. Here is another way to look at it.

CEO Role – External Focus	Management Role – Internal Focus
"The buck stops here"—(accountability)	The results are mine—(responsibility)
Influencer	Problem solver
Strategic (thinking two to three years out)	Tactical (next three to six months)
Trains people to think and then delegates	Manages the details (all about the checklist)
Visionary	Manages the process
Optimistic: everything is an opportunity	Realistic: manages business risk
Moral compass	Follow-up
Good listener	Takes care of customers
Knowledgeable and wants to share it	Takes care of employees
Resource allocation: people, money, priorities	Takes care of suppliers
Voice of the firm: works *on* the Business	Works *in* the Business
Bottom Line: *Focus is on increasing the value of the organization (strategy)*	Bottom Line: *Focus is on the efficient and effective operation of the organization (tactics)*

Stay In CEO Mode With Your Strategic Lens

Today CEOs face an unprecedented degree of complexity that is constantly reshaping the business landscape. To successfully execute new strategies, organizations must accelerate the pace of building critical senior-level alignment and ownership around the strategic direction[20]. Developing a strategic lens and the right culture are the two vital tools a CEO needs to build alignment and avoid becoming the HR department.

We know you did not start your business to be the head of HR. Yet your people are complex and you care. Working hard day in and day out to fulfill a company's goals takes a lot out of staff. As leaders, it is our job to make sure our people are nurtured and cared for so they can stay strong and thrive. Just like a plant needs watering, sunlight, and pruning, so do people and organizations. Use your culture and your strategic lens to make the difference.

Culture tells staff if their decisions and behaviors are aligned to the firm's mores. It shortcuts how much feedback is needed in the firm.

The strategic lens tool helps staff to identify and name the root problems. To help them make better decisions aligned to the strategy.

Bottom line, going through Transition can be an exciting and sometimes frustrating time in that it offers you a golden opportunity for a very bright future. It is exciting because the business is finally getting the kind of traction needed to really grow.

It is frustrating in that the revenue growth and leadership structure needs to change. Because there is a decided lack of predictability at this stage with your leadership team it is ridiculously hard to plan. It seems the ground upon which you are trying to build keeps shifting like quicksand, whether it is the fluctuations in revenue, production, or staffing that is experienced. As CEO, your task is to trust and build a solid strategic lens.

Key Takeaways:

1. Know your role as CEO and stay in your lane (do not fall for blunder three or four)

2. Use your strategic lens to stay in strategy. And use metrics to show if the company is on track.

3. Invite and train others to think and lead like you. Allow them to help you solve the big hairy problems.

4. Use culture to help staff make better decisions and, thus, create less work for the executive.

PART III

CHANGE THE GAME: BE BOLDER

7
SECRET SAUCE PART ONE:
ALIGN THE SPINE

"Great growth isn't a function of luck.
It is a function of aligned efforts."

The first part of this book explains what stops a company from breaking the $10 million growth barrier. It introduced a new concept called Transition and how that messes with an emerging firm's plans for growth. We also explained how Transition causes a company to fall prey to four blunders, keeping them stuck in a Groundhog Day loop.

The second part of this book outlines a system to increase your firm's value, not just the size of your firm: the Predictable Profitability System.

Part three is the bonus—what it will take to keep that growth happening every year (aka acceleration). Included in this system are three tools to help differentiate your company from your competition. They are:

- A way of aligning: the strategic lens and the culture, and defining the right problems
- A way of thinking: the genius and strategic thinking
- A way of accelerating growth: replicating success

Why Alignment Matters

Simply put, alignment exists when a company delivers what the customer wants and how they want it—profitably. Internally, it looks like a shared company mindset that your staff and leadership team have to the goals and objectives of the firm. Externally, it looks like *buy-in*. Both are an agreement to why the company exists—its story.

What causes 70 percent of staff to be unhappy, per the 2022 State of the Global Workplace, Gallup Poll, is misalignment to how (not what) their company delivers its product/service and feeling like they cannot do anything about it. Our clients noticed when they aligned staff to the firm's goals and objectives (by defining the company mindset) profitability and engagement went up.

To achieve alignment, you need to get some things straight. Like your story. Like your staffs' thinking (developing a strategic lens to find/solve problems and make better decisions). Like your metrics—what you measure to determine if the company is on or off track. And how you deliver services to the marketplace.

To maintain alignment, you need to couple the leadership element, particularly the decision-making process (strategic lens), to the profit element, specifically a new way of thinking.

And you need a reliable tool, like culture to inform you, the leader, if you and your staff are aligned to your story and your processes.

Get Your Story Straight

While it might sound simple, getting your story straight is anything but trivial. Your story has an external component like why your company exists and what it wants to provide to the marketplace. It also has an internal component based on how it delivers and who the company is comprised of. Having the external view and the internal perspective aligned is how companies go from ordinary to bold.

As your company has grown you may have noticed that your original story has been added to and perhaps modified as staff inject their interpretation and beliefs. There is value in documenting a story that can be relatable and retold accurately by everyone, clients and staff alike. That kind of clarity creates engagement with staff and resonance with prospective clients.

Create a story that inspires all (staff, vendors, and clients) to want to participate. Paint a bright future informing all where you are heading and what they can expect from you (your why). Define what you do best, who your ideal client is, and the problem you are solving for them. Clearly articulate your values, culture, and purpose.

It is not so important that your people can recite the story word for word. What is more important is that these concepts drive desired behaviors and decisions. In other words, your staff embody the story. So that when it comes time for them to make a difficult decision, better choices are easier for them to discern.

Meet Luke

Luke wants more clients. Even though his business is highly technical, and Luke is one of the best in his industry, he is not well-known to his potential client base. He wants something that will attract those prospects. He thinks the best way to do that is with a website. He hires a marketing firm that revamps his firm's website, whose objective is to attract clients with new website messaging.

Often, a marketing consultant will include in their process an exercise to determine values. Luke's consultant used the filter or lens: what will attract the customer? But values ought to reflect the company, not what we think someone wants to hear. When our values are aligned to what is most important to us, they will attract the clients who want the same thing.

In Luke's case that filter created a misalignment between his company's values (internal focus) and the marketing message (external focus).

When Luke put the outward facing values (customer service, quality, and collaboration) on his website and not the values his firm is based on (innovation, excellence, integrity, and flexibility) he had trouble attracting the right kind of client.

Oddly, Luke noticed that his staff started creating a more collaborative client experience (website message) rather than providing the expert solution (the company message). This caused inefficiencies for the staff and frustration for the client. In Luke's line of work the client wants the correct and best solution (he is a patent attorney) rather than figuring it out with a specialist. Picture you have been diagnosed with cancer and the doctor, instead of informing you of your best options says, "Well, you have cancer. Where should we start?" Imagine the fear and frustration.

Needless to say, Luke was frustrated, and a bit confused with the unintended consequence that his staff aligned to the outward facing values and changed their work approach.

It did not take long after re-aligning the website message to be consistent with the internal values, for productivity and profits to return to Luke's firm. The net result for Luke was the company tripled in size over the next three years and its profitability increased to a net 20 percent. In a nutshell, staff naturally align to what resonates with them and produce accordingly.

Can you see that neither messaging is wrong but when there is a lack of alignment externally to what the company is selling and internally how it delivers, efficiencies go down and lower profitability follows suit quickly? It drives the wrong customer to you. So how do you find to attract the right customer to you?

What The Customer Wants

A great place to start is: What problem is your company solving? Then determine who wants what you are selling. The best markets to be selling into are those that truly need what you are offering and are willing to place a value on your product. That affects how much you can charge and how profitable you can be. And it eliminates blunder one (any sale is a good sale).

Next describe your ideal client—their characteristics, their industry, what they want from you and how to reach them. Now evaluate how many of your current clients fit the description. If less than 20 percent of your clients are ideal, review how you deliver your services and whether you have clearly defined what problem you are solving for the customer. Ask yourself if you have an abundance of marginally profitable sales (blunder one).

Finally ask why and what your clients are buying? Please do not assume you know the answer unless you have asked. When companies like Starbucks, McDonalds and Apple asked, here is what they heard.

Starbucks: a shared experience. Their location and interior design matters. McDonalds: consistency. Customers wanted to go anywhere in the world and have the hamburger taste the same. Process and suppliers are essential. Apple: the best and most innovative solutions. They need to consistently deliver cutting edge, reliable solutions. Well-tested, creative ideas are needed.

These companies aligned their story, their product and their delivery system to their ideal client. Make sure lots of people think your solution is the best answer to their problem.

Get Your People's Mindset Straight

Every company has a mindset, an established set of attitudes, outlook, and way of decision-making. It informs staff on how the company processes information and solves problems. And it is either explicit (documented) or implicit (implied). As your company grows and you add more people, you may find that a range of ideas and opinions surface. Your job is to get everyone onto the same page by defining your company mindset. It is done through your story, your why, your culture. If these are not documented your staff will have to guess, making alignment to decision-making much harder.

Start by defining your leadership element (your culture, values, why). Then define your strategic lens (the root problem to solve) and your genius thinking (your company's unique solution). With your company mindset established, you can create a strong and vibrant business that can scale.

Meet Neel

When Neel first became our client, his company had a net profit of 5 percent, which was not enough money to scale a business. The way his industry worked, projects were written as cost-plus contracts with a 10 percent capped fee. Seven percent was guaranteed. The last 3 percent were earned based on performance.

Neel's firm was consistently having cost overruns, costing them that last 3 percent. This company knew how to manage and deliver projects. So why were they running over in the millions of dollars on each project and why wasn't the team overly concerned? Neel got curious.

He started with bringing clarity to the problem with his management team. He used a strong visual that he named the Death Spiral to explain what was happening: they would be awarded a contract. They would continue to have overruns (which would be paid because it was a cost-plus contract). They would forfeit the 3 percent bonus. And eventually the agencies would blacklist the firm because they kept running over on the projects. And then the company would die.

Then he waited. A *big* lightbulb went off with the team.

They understood the story. They thought running over budget did not really matter because they would not be out-of-pocket on expenses. But they did not understand the impact overruns had on future jobs and that the 3 percent bonus was lost profits. Now they understood what was at stake.

Next, they needed to bring their strategic lens to the problem of overruns. They discovered most of the overruns occurred in the first 25 percent of the job. Shifting their focus, they implemented better reporting and processes to enhance performance. They started earning the bonus. That meant staff's 401ks saw more money going in. And the executive team could now talk about expanding the business, which they did in the next three years, more than doubling revenue from $30 million to $65 million. More jobs, more opportunities, more fun.

Neel's leadership team thought they planned correctly. They thought they were aligned. Their profitability told a different story. And, while it may seem obvious in the retelling, for those in the field it was not easy to see without an outside perspective. Defining your strategic lens will help.

Get Your Metrics Straight

High performers want to know how the company is doing and if what they are doing is adding value. And they want to know how they can improve. Tying metrics to the plan, gives your staff the tool to measure their own performance. The bonus, metrics help you, as the CEO, to see where and when to bring more resources to weak areas.

There is an old business adage that says "You cannot manage what you do not measure". We would say that if you do not measure, how do you even know where you are?

There are endless things to measure in a company. Metrics are designed to give a quick snapshot of what is going on and where to focus attention. The trick is to find only five to seven that provide the best information to see trends and make better decisions. Some organizations measure too many things. Others not enough. The right question is, are you measuring the things that will help you make better decisions, faster?

We believe metrics are the glue that binds together your culture with your plan. It is the context for accountability that supports performance and generates results. It is the dashboard that helps you see at a glance how you are doing. It also helps your people answer the all-important question: "How am I doing?"

Some questions to ponder:

- Are your metrics aligned to the culture of the company?
- Do your metrics measure progress towards your why?
- Do your metrics highlight how you are doing against your strategic plan?
- Do they set off a red flag when you stray from the strategy?

In conclusion, if you want your company to be more valuable be clear about your story. Then align it to your decision-making (embedded in your leadership element). Then fine-tune your foundation.

Key Takeaways:

1. Your story matters. If you do not give your staff something to be excited about, they will create drama (bad drama) to have excitement.

2. Alignment matters. It causes performance to rise. Make sure your leadership element and your foundation are in sync as they are the cornerstones to creating a scalable company.

3. To correctly measure performance, fine-tune your metrics and culture.

4. Your company mindset is told through your story and your culture.

8
SECRET SAUCE PART TWO: THINK LIKE A GENIUS

"The thinking that got you here will not get you there."
Marshall Goldsmith

"There" is to become a professionally managed company for the new entrepreneur. You have learned that using your strategic lens to identify issues changes what needs to be solved. And that, naturally, changes the solutions available to solve the problem. It changes your experience as an owner and the destiny of your company.

In other words, to change the game and win the entrepreneurial lotto begins with changing the perspective you had at the pre-professional stage of "more sales" to that of finding what the market craves from your business (your S-factor). New perspectives open up new ways of thinking. In this chapter we demonstrate how to develop these new ways of thinking and turn them into extraordinary results. Then we will show you how to use the tool called culture to replicate that thinking throughout your company.

As our clients keep telling us, for their company to win big it requires they have a cornerstone that could support and promote the growth they want. Their cornerstone was built upon three premises from which we built our Predictable Profitability System: their foundation, their leadership, and their profitability. As you know, a stable foundation—systems, processes, and infrastructure—means your firm can reliably deliver your solution to the marketplace. The second leg, a solid leadership element defines and aligns how it delivers your solution through your story, your why, and your culture.

The third leg of a company cornerstone is building a way of thinking that produces out-of-the-box results, the essential components of the profitability element. Couple this cornerstone with acceleration and now you have a company that can consistently, predictably scale.

Our Predictable Profitability System provides a new point of view on performance, profitability, and stability while still mitigating risk. It turns the industry norm way of thinking that focuses on processes and sales as the chief components of growing on its head. It uses your S-factor to turn market buy-in into a high demand for your product. It provides an agile approach to decision-making that allows your company to pivot quickly, turning your answers into simple, elegant solutions. And, it provides tools needed to evaluate your performance.

A New Way Of Thinking

Redefining a problem (and specifically not including confirmation or complexity bias), opens the door to unique solutions.

In other words, how problems are defined and solved in your organization sets the tone for developing the kind of thinking that will differentiate your firm. We call this genius thinking.

> "Most geniuses—especially those who lead others— prosper not by deconstructing intricate complexities but by exploiting unrecognized simplicities."
>
> — *Andy Benoit*

Genius thinking, then, embodies both effectiveness and simplicity.

Effectiveness: the ability to consistently produce the results we intend. Steve Jobs was effective in his first round of running Apple. He learned the art of simplicity at Pixar. When he combined the two upon his return to Apple, it became the largest and most profitable company in the world.

The point is not to be enmeshed in focusing on the hard stuff but rather to look at the situation differently. In school we are taught to spend time mastering the subjects we have trouble with rather than exploiting what comes naturally and easily to us[21]. That makes us think we are supposed to focus on and conquer the tough stuff. We are suggesting that maybe a different perspective might help. What if we focused instead on what comes easiest to us? What if we focused on a simple (not the same as easy) solution? In Aikido, we are taught to use the energy of the opponent (by joining with them) rather than putting up resistance to block them. That is what we are saying genius thinking is all about.

Simple: Doing simple well takes practice and focus. Most of us think more is better. More explanation is better. More data is better. More color. More complexity. Yet, more complexity can help us avoid addressing our issues. Today we are all bombarded with more information every day, all day. Is it helping? Have our lives become simpler because of all the information or more complex? Did you know that with the advent of the internet (1995) new information went from doubling every one hundred years to doubling every twelve to thirteen months? Today new information doubles every twelve hours. It is not possible for you to stay ahead of all the information coming at you. Not even in your field of expertise.

Consider that 'more is better' is the wrong premise. What if less is better? And how do we manage with less when information is changing so rapidly? Consider that much of what is coming at you is noise—a distraction. Your job is to filter out that noise and focus on what matters.

When Leonardo da Vinci said, "Simplicity is the ultimate sophistication," he didn't mean take a short cut down the path of least resistance, balancing your work and personal life by giving it equal priorities, or set more attainable, smart goals. He meant to find a solution that embodies the results in the simplest way possible, with no compromise. The key is no compromise. It means only one thing may be a priority now. And not later.

> "Life is really simple, but we insist on making it complicated."— Confucius

Genius tip #1: Simple means focusing on only the most important facet of a situation, problem, or issue. Complexity is the opposite. Something complex is not necessarily hard, but it is multi-faceted. A metric based on more than three factors is complex, while a metric with one or two variables is simple. Many factors can introduce chaos or noise. And that noise tends to mask the true problem. Your job as leader is to cut through the noise. Cull it down to the two or three most important points. Train your staff to do so too.

Genius tip #2: Chaos is often confused with being complex but is not; it is only random. Engaging with chaos can help us find the elegant solutions. How to do that, is simple. Start by looking for the patterns just below the surface of the problem you are trying to solve. Those will guide you to the root cause. Once you have the root cause in hand, start to look at the nuances. Which matter? Which do not? Use the nuances that matter to adjust, refine, and then pivot. Think of it like sailing—constantly adjusting to the wind, the waves.

It takes focus and effort!

Genius tip #3: Learn to cut through all the noise and chaos the company is throwing at you right now. Look for the core, the essence of what is causing the disruption. And focus there. Solve that. Be the genius there. All this can be learned.

Meet Jacob

Jacob runs a highly successful marketing firm, one of the three largest in San Diego. We met at a networking event and over drinks he started complaining about his team and how they were not producing. Rosemary restated what she heard him say and offered a simple solution. He exploded. After he took a breath in his rant she asked, "Was I wrong?". His answer astonished her. He said that that was beside the point. The point was that the solution couldn't be that easy.

In other words, he thought the problem to solve was more complex because he had not solved it yet. And because Rosemary did not have the company bias (not being an employee) she could hear clearly what he was saying the problem was and then she offered a way to solve it, simply and elegantly.

The trick is to be able to distance yourself (become an observer) enough to hear the root problem. That's where a coach or a group like Vistage, TAB, or Renaissance (to name a few) can really help. Once you have mastered being an observer, you will have luck on your side. You will seem almost clairvoyant in your observations and insights. And you will then know the best place to start in making changes. Find your own way to separate the noise from the real issues, whether that means to talk it out with someone who is not in your firm. Or write out a process flow chart. Or take a walk. Just separate the noise from the root issue.

The Barriers to Genius Thinking

One of our favorite definitions of genius is: *the test of a first-rate intelligence is the ability to hold two opposing ideas in the mind at the same time and still retain the ability to function.*[22]

One way to think differently is to avoid looking for the most complex solution like Jacob did.

Most of us, when faced with two competing hypotheses, tend to choose the more complex one, eliminating the simple solution. It means that when we need to solve a problem, we may ignore simple solutions—thinking "that is too easy"—and instead, favor complex ones. Complex options tend to have the most assumptions. There is a name for that (have you noticed that there is a name for practically everything?) and it is called "complexity bias".

Scientists have found that complexity bias is a logic fallacy that leads us to give undue credence to complex concepts. If we can interrupt that cycle, we will begin to create brilliant solutions. Yes, we need to hear all the issues and then discern the core issue. From there we need to seek the simplest, cleanest answer that addresses all the issues. Here is what the professionals say about cognitive biases:[23]

> *Most of our cognitive biases occur to save mental energy. For example, confirmation bias enables us to avoid the effort associated with updating our beliefs. We stick to our existing opinions and ignore information that contradicts them. Availability bias is a means of avoiding the effort of*

considering everything we know about a topic...complexity bias is, in fact, another cognitive shortcut. By opting for impenetrable solutions, we sidestep the need to understand. Of the fight-or-flight responses, complexity bias is the flight response. It is a means of turning away from a problem or concept and labeling it as too confusing. If you think something is harder than it is, you surrender your responsibility to understand it.

Faced with too much information on a particular topic or task, we see it as more complex than it is. Often, understanding the fundamentals will get us most of the way there. Software developers often find that 90 percent of the code for a project takes about half the allocated time. The remaining 10 percent takes the other half. Writing—and any other sort of creative work—is much the same. When we succumb to Complexity Bias, we are focusing too long the tricky 10 percent and ignoring the easy 90 percent.

Said another way, it is our tendency to overthink a situation. To believe, like Jacob, that the solution must be difficult doesn't allow us to develop a simple, elegant solution. Our job, as leaders, is to clear out the noise and help our staff find the simple elegant solution.

Genius tip #4 When faced with a problem, identify and start with the easy 90 percent. Seek outside help for the last 10 percent. Ask other CEOs what they hear you say the 10 percent problem is. Then ask people to challenge your thinking. From there you will find better solutions, faster. You will become known as a genius thinker.

Key Takeaways

1. Think differently.

   - Define the problem you are solving without confirmation bias.

   - Use perspective to get out of your typical thinking pattern.

   - Practice simplicity to avoid complexity bias and the complicated, expensive solutions.

2. Change your leadership element to encourage and reward new thinking.

3. Because we all have inherent bias in our thinking, it helps to have our thoughts challenged by third parties not invested in the company.

9

SECRET SAUCE PART THREE: CURATE YOUR CULTURE

"Culture informs the leader how good a job they are doing."

The vehicle that aligns thinking and decision-making is called culture. It can also support genius thinking (out-of-the-box decisions that propel growth).

Further, smart business leaders use the culture tool as a feedback loop to determine how effectively their mandates are executed. Any misalignment in how a plan is executed will be revealed simply by looking at the culture. Any wobble causes performance to suffer. And just like that profitability becomes unstable.

Culture, used properly, becomes part of your secret sauce to success. It is a tool that teaches everyone in your firm what will and will not be tolerated. It informs staff on how to make decisions that align with the boss. It is the foundation upon which a leader builds better performance.

The Organic Evolution of Culture

Culture is the beliefs, behaviors and values that determine how a company's employees and management interact, handle, and make business decisions internally and externally. If a corporate culture is implied and not expressly defined it will develop organically over time and will be based on the cumulative traits of the people the company hires. Culture exists in all companies, whether it is formally defined or not. As your enterprise became more successful and stable, certain behaviors became the norm. Whether you realized it or not, set out to design it or not, what grew out of this is your organization's culture. This became "our way of doing things" and was taught to new people as they came onboard, thereby perpetuating and expanding the organic culture of the organization.

In his book *Organizational Culture and Leadership*[24], Edgar H. Schein offered this perspective on how your organization's culture evolves.

> *The culture of a group can now be defined as a pattern of shared basic assumptions that was learned by a group as it solved its problems of external adaptation and internal integration, that has worked well enough to be considered valid and, therefore, to be taught to new members as the correct way to perceive, think, and feel in relation to those problems.*

Schein makes this point, "The bottom line for leaders is that if they do not become conscious of the cultures in which they are embedded, those cultures will manage them. Cultural understanding is desirable for all of us, but it is essential to leaders if they are to lead."[25]

Culture is an essential element to being an extraordinary leader and changing the game in your favor.

Culture By Definition

Here is a brief description of the four cultures we use and how we work with them. They are loosely based on the work of Steve Schneider[26]. This model helps give a common language and understanding around a complex matter. We are not saying that there are only four ways to define culture. You can use any word you want if you consistently apply it across your why, values, decision-making and metrics. We offer this as an easy way to discuss, evaluate, and integrate culture.

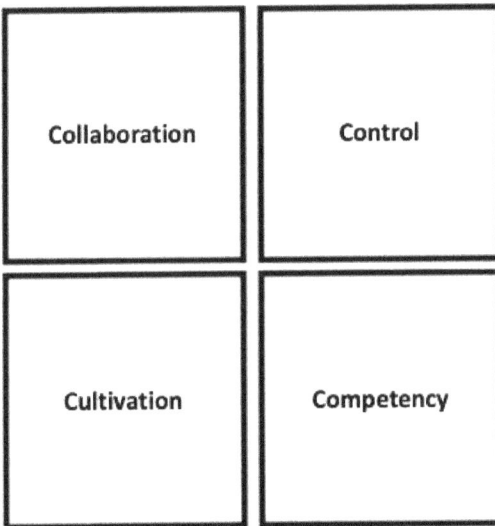

Collaboration	Control
Cultivation	Competency

Collaboration: A Clustered Team Approach. The point of collaboration is to include the customer in the decision-making process of product or service delivery. Think of the customer as a team member, even though they are not your employee. Vigorous debate is encouraged, and consensus is required with all decisions. Because of that, the hierarchy is flat, flexible, and adaptable. The sales process drives agreement and win-wins between the customer and company. Team members are empowered to make decisions that support what the customer wants. This is all about the customer, not about process. Success is a happy customer. In a word: team.

Control: Hierarchal, Data Driven Approach. The point of control is to provide excellent and efficient service delivery. Decision-making is a top-down process based on rank, authority, and data. This culture is process-heavy, designed to execute the company's goals through compliance and data. The organizational hierarchy is clearly defined and documented. The sales process defines what the company will and will not provide. It has clearly defined methods for vetting new customers and how it makes decisions objectively. It is not about people. It is about process and data. Success is an efficient and excellent execution of process. In a word: process.

Competency: The Best Solution Based On Expertise Approach. The point of competency is to gather the best of the best and leverage their expertise, knowledge, connections to determine the most effective solution for a problem. This culture is known for its ability to make the best decisions quickly at the individual level. The expectation is that the customer will implement the company's recommendations. The sales process is designed to find the customers that need their expertise and are willing to pay top dollar. This is all about individual excellence and being recognized as being "the best". Teams are used to leverage knowledge. Success is finding and providing the best solution for the customer's problem. In a word: expert.

Cultivation: Inspiring The Fulfillment Of A Purpose Approach. The point of cultivation is the growth and development of the individual + the company + the client. There is an alignment to something bigger than just profits. There is a purpose or why that must be fulfilled. Decisions are made that support a big picture. Processes are guideposts to inform all to think strategically and deliver the why. Teams are formed to identify, train, and capitalize on the best each member brings to the table. The sales process focuses on uncovering the big picture. It involves learning and an exchange of ideas. Success is defined as making a difference. In a word: purpose.

Nature Versus Nurture

Earlier we said your company's culture reflects who you are as a leader and the staff you invested in along the way. We believe a leader has a natural leadership style. You either insist on making all the decisions yourself (control) or you like to check in with a group of trusted people to make decisions (collaboration) or you do research to find the expert (a person, book, or paper) and solicit their advice (competency) or you base your decision on some grand idea that you are committed to seeing in the world (cultivation).

When we first met Isaac, it was clear that he has big ideas about changing his industry (cultivation). Yet his business is set up in the control culture: hierarchal in nature because he does not know how to manage people without many rules. Until he does, his big ideas will need to wait. And he needs to hire good rule followers.

Some industries are naturally better suited to certain cultures. For example, CPA and attorney firms naturally fit into a competency culture (they are the resident expert). Marketing firms naturally fit into a collaboration culture (the customer is part of the design process). But it does not mean that it has to be that way.

You, as the leader, can change to any culture—it just takes time. The only thing is, please be consistent. Your staff will sniff out and raise a ruckus anywhere you, your processes, your rewards, your compensation package, your team are inconsistent. Not intentionally, mind you. It is just the nature of humans to know when something is asymmetrical or out of balance. The gut instinct is to resist inconsistencies.

How To Use Culture

First decide which culture appeals to you. Read the descriptions and determine which you prefer. Next see how you have organized your company. Are your processes and metrics aligned to the culture you chose? If they aren't, pick how you have organized the firm. Next make sure that the values you have picked align to your chosen culture.

Most people apply standard metrics to their sales teams and to their staff. Instead use the metrics for each culture.

Your metrics need to measure the what, how, and yield. The *what* is what one produces. The *how* is how one operates and delivers. The *yield* is the quality output. Here is a quick guide to metrics by culture:

Collaboration Culture

Because the focus is on the team and relationships, reward team (not individual) efforts. With your sales team, you want to reward where they bring in strategic alliances or engage the rest of the team in landing a sale. With staff, reward where they have developed other staff. Create awards and bonuses documenting an employee supporting another. Design mentor programs. Building or maintaining relationships is an important metric in this culture. Customer retention is a strong metric for your sales staff.

How Mary Incorporated The Collaboration Culture.

Mary's law firm was based on a culture of collaboration. To fulfill that, each equity partner had a stint as managing partner so they all understood the job and could make similar decisions. Then they created a compensation plan that rewarded team effort. Typically, attorney firms measure and reward three things:

1. How many hours worked were billed to the client (called utilization rate)?

2. How many of those hours did the client actually pay (called the realization rate)? The industry standard is an 8 percent write-off or 92 percent realization for attorneys. Anything better than 92 percent collection is a big win.

3. How much new business did you bring in?

Mary's firm measured and reported:

1. Firmwide utilization and realization rates
2. Profit contribution by case.
3. Professional staff education. Any staff person who attended a seminar gave a short presentation to the firm on key points.
4. Any non-professional service (business development, serving as managing partner or staff development) was compensated to cover lost billable time.

Innovative and it rewarded team development.

Control Culture

The focus is the company and how *consistently* it performs. SOPs (processes and procedures) are vital. They are the backbone of the organization. Metrics are tied to results and data. Newsletters should highlight well-structured programs.

How Bobby Incorporated The Control Culture

In this culture it is all about data and processes. Bobby's contracting company measures accidents. In their company newsletter they publish how many days they go accident free; they lose a lot of time when there is an accident. OSHA requires employees visit a medical professional when there is an accident. Because of the time it takes to go to an offsite urgent care the staff are reluctant to report minor incidents.

To encourage staff health and reduce down time Bobby chose to build an on-site urgent care. He hired a nurse and made an onsite medical office. Several things happened. First their accident-free metric was met. They went to zero accidents for twelve months (from an average of one a week). Next, staff were offered the flu shot on site so sick time also went down. And as a result, productivity when up. And that drove profitability up. Powerful.

Competency Culture

This culture is about individual excellence. Creating friendly competition is needed and wanted in this culture. Comparing how a person is doing relative to others matters to the people in this culture. Please note, collaboration folks do not like lists that show who is excelling and who is not (obviously because in their mind it is NOT about individual performance and only the team). Competency staff prefer to focus on individual excellence. Important metrics are: utilization and realization performance, and individual ranking on the team.

How Jane Incorporated The Competency Culture

Jane's company provides training, actionable intelligence, and data support for the military. One of the company's core values is excellence in everything they do and touch. So Jane created a wall of fame in the reception area. Every quarter seven staff, each representing one of the seven core values of the firm, have their picture hung in a frame in the reception area describing the value they modeled. Staff contributions are talked about at every company meeting. At their annual gatherings, the best of the best are brought to the front of the room, in front of their families, recognized and given a cash bonus. The impact is that productivity and profitability increased (to 20 percent net). The market caught wind of their excellent service, gaining access to bigger and better projects and the best candidates for hire. Revenue and profitability skyrocketed allowing them to buy up smaller competition. Genius.

Cultivation Culture

This is a learning culture so you want to incorporate and reward learning. That can be as simple as having a budget for education that staff can access. While other cultures (like competency) can also have an education budget, this culture encourages personal development, not just technical development. Many organizations that are cultivation oriented incorporate an internal "university model". This system is designed to train the staff on what is important for the individual and the company to excel. It could be conflict resolution, communications, office skills like Excel, Word, PowerPoint, writing, and presentation skills. You decide.

How Chris Incorporated The Cultivation Culture

Chris created a company university originally to train his staff to give better client presentations. They even had a mascot (the hedgehog). He went so far as to invite outside guests once a year to listen to the presentations and evaluate the speakers. Because Chris's firm was small and his exec team was with him from the beginning, they did not have the leadership expertise they needed. So he put one of the staff in charge of the university. He put another staff member in charge of their charity fundraiser. A third staff person oversaw their well-being program. Each learned how to manage and lead a team and produce results. By managing a project where it was "safe to fail" they learned essential leadership skills without impacting revenue-bearing activities. It had the added benefit of allowing him to evaluate their leadership capacity. Brilliant.

The Red Flags of Culture

A misaligned culture costs time and money.

In accounting there is a saying that goes like this: it is better to be consistently wrong than it is to be inconsistently right. Culture operates the same way. Consistency matters. And when there are inconsistencies in applying culture, like the metrics are in one culture and the leadership is in another, it creates mischief in the company.

Here are some red flags our clients report that impact critical resources the firm has little to spare:

> Internally: Employee disengagement. Gossip abounds. Staff turnover is on the rise. Productivity and performance start to slip. Staff are frustrated, confused, or resigned leading to inefficiencies. That affects profitability, and that impacts cash flow.

> Externally: Lost business opportunities. With uncertain, unaligned, or unclear messaging, potential clients hesitate, and opportunities start slipping through the cracks. Or worse, you attract clients who are equally misaligned, and they demand more time and attention with less revenue leading to lower profits that affect cash flow.

An aligned culture attracts better staff and cash flow

In their book *The Progress Principle,* Harvard Business School professor Teresa Amabile and independent researcher Steven Kramer found that the strongest organizations nurtured their employees' inner work lives by allowing them to make progress in meaningful work. Your culture is the platform to do that.

By now you recognize the importance of culture because it not only defines your company's shared beliefs (explicit or implicit) which drives the behaviors and decisions your staff make but it is also a metric you can use to measure staff satisfaction. If your culture is positive and inspiring, it will add to your staff's motivation. That adds to the component of staff engagement which causes your firm to elevate to an expanded level of performance.

That extra bump in performance is a game changer because it fixes cash flow issues and attracts the kind of staff you want. You will experience extremely high staff morale and elevated staff engagement. Both personal and company goals and objectives are met or exceeded. Productivity increases results in a more collaborative and cooperative team approach. Profitability goes up. Cash flow works and exciting new alliances and opportunities present themselves. People are having fun. And that attracts better clients. The kind of client we all dream about who pay their bills quickly and bring better projects for us to work on.

Key Takeaways:

1. Align your performance metrics and goals to your culture.

2. Culture is designed to show how aligned your staff are to you, your goals and how the company is executing on them.

3. Culture will keep your staff or kick them out. If you have high turnover, look at your culture for answers.

4. Create succession plans to grow staff that are aligned to the culture.

10
WHAT'S NEXT?

"Doing the same thing over and over again is the definition of insanity (and stagnation). Change your strategy now."

Putting it all together, you got a glimpse of how Transition changes the rules of achieving predictable, sustainable growth. You saw the pitfalls other leaders fell into when they tried to handle growth in typical ways (the four blunders). It is obvious that without a new approach to defining and resolving business issues a barrier to success is formed.

We offered several strategy tools to define a new approach to success. These tools have a dual purpose. First is to help break the growth barrier. Second is to create consistent, sustainable growth. When you and your staff reliably focus on the big picture (the strategy), it facilitates the advancement of genius solutions. That builds confidence in the entire team. And just like that 'Bolder' becomes a possibility.

We incorporated all this into our Predictable Profitability System, which visually shows the building blocks for all companies. More importantly, it shows the relationship between how the building block components work together. It is designed to help you out of Transition faster, making bolder possible.

Bolder: The Art Of The Transition Pivot

Starting a company is fun and exciting. It challenges its leader to be better. And then comes the opportunity to be bigger. Unfortunately for 80 percent of business owners, this is where they are stopped. This is where they fail because they did not recognize they were in Transition and did not learn the art of the pivot to exit it. We want to change all that.

Pivoting is a dramatic change in policy, position, or strategy. In business it means changing some aspect of its core framework. This entire book is designed to teach you the art of the pivot—knowing where to start and what to change.

Companies in their first Transition (revenue between $3 million and $10 million) must learn to pivot into a consistent, profitable growth mindset with the object of "scaling a company". It could be how the company delivers its service, or what it offers to the client. It could involve greater automation, better client interfaces, or better staff who have aligned processes and decision-making. It could be one or a multiple of these.

The first Transition's problem is that it can be exhausting to know where to start. That wears down the leader. It can leave the owner believing that getting bigger means more exhausting work. Not true. CEOs at the professionally managed stage call it the Land of Plenty. There is enough time, money, staff, clients, resources. Anything that comes up can be handled by a team and not just by you. Better thinking and solutions arise when staff are aligned to a common outcome. In other words, it is a *lot* less stressful.

In the second Transition where companies have exceeded $10 million in sales, the pivot usually comes down to how your product/service is delivered. When CDs were introduced into the marketplace it changed *how* music was delivered to the customer. All vinyl record companies either pivoted or went out of business. This second pivot then is a focused, tight adjustment to how you get your product/service into the hands of your clients.

Remember, the purpose or intention of Transition is for you to discover (or refine) what your firm is truly best at and sell only that. Why does that matter? Because a pivot of some kind will be needed every seven or so years. Get your staff used to rethinking your business framework to keep your business fresh and growing.

We want to leave you with a final story that puts it all together.

Meet Jack

Jack wants to scale (break the $10 million barrier).

Stop and Do a Scalability Assessment

Start with your foundation and leadership elements.

First determine the maximum load the foundation elements can absorb before major upgrades are required. Look at the accounting system, customer relationship software, IT systems, staffing needs (like adding a high-level management executive). If the foundation is not solid enough to integrate a consistent, large influx of revenue without breaking, stop. Repair the foundation.

Next determine if the leadership team's thinking is aligned. Your culture will inform you. If it is not aligned, stop, and define your strategic lens.

When Jack assessed his foundation, he saw that it was at its breaking point. His infrastructure (accounting system, IT system, and hiring system) were about to collapse. He was getting complaints from his customers that their bills were incorrect and untimely, causing a cash flow problem. His HR team was new and unprepared to handle the influx of new hires they needed to grow at the pace Jack wanted. They needed more of everything: staff, processes, software, and hardware. New software to sort and manage resumes. A new onboarding system to expedite assimilation of new staff. A new method for determining fit for a position, and a means to find the best candidates. Jack has no executive management team (he needs a CFO, an HR exec, and his COO is not making the grade). Without a well-defined strategic lens to focus everyone in the right direction, costly mistakes will happen.

Jack needed to identify the best place to start.

The Right Starting Point

Most want to start with adding sales. But adding sales to a system at its breaking point will only exacerbate the problem or worse, cause a company to implode. It is common in Transition that several immediate, real problems make competing demands on time, money, and other resources—all of which are in short supply at this phase. Use a Scalability Assessment to determine the right place to start for your company. It is essential if you want to avoid costly mistakes. The right starting point usually is the Leadership-Profit relationship.

Initially, Jack wanted to solve his cash flow problem by adding revenue. He figured once he had money, he could solve all the other problems (blunder one - sales cures all ills). Yet if he does, it may break his company. Jack was facing a paradox—competing priorities for resources.

The Paradox Solution

Competing priorities for resources often cause an executive to turn to growing sales as the solution, particularly when cash is needed. Seek instead to increase profits, through better staff performance and profitable sales (not just increasing the top line revenue).

When Jack reviewed his Predictable Profitability System, he saw he needed to do two things. First develop a strategic lens with the management team and then introduce a performance mindset to become profitable. His leadership-profit relationship was out of alignment.

While Jack's team said they were aligned, (he got lots of head nods when he laid out the goals), the results showed something different. He was losing clients and profitability— two big signs of misalignment.

Jack has two problems: a foundation that will break with additional sales and a leadership element that is not producing profits. When facing that kind of complexity start with enhancing alignment. Your Strategic Lens will do that.

Strategic Lens

Articulating a strategic lens for staff creates alignment with the goals and how the company fulfills those goals. It eliminates confusion that may arise when there are conflicting priorities or staff do not understand the direction management has chosen. Your strategic lens teaches everyone how to uncover the problem that needs solving and then better ways to resolve those matters in alignment with the company mindset.

Jack's Big Results

Jack's project management team were convinced the executives were going after the wrong business. Once they understood what the company could and could not go after, and what their scalability factor was, they aligned. Jack's project management team picked up $7 million in projects on existing jobs for small contract add-ons that increased customer service and added profit since they did not take more staff or time to deliver on.

Staff buy-in to the future and their scalability factor was so high it triggered a market buzz. Old customers who had taken them off their bid lists added them back. And that turned into $13 million in new client projects by year's end. In the first year they had increased revenue by 37 percent without their business development person closing a single deal. Profitability increased to 20 percent (from breakeven) within the first year.

Alignment causes profitability. With profits Jack could tackle the next problem: creating a high functioning management team. He started by hiring a CFO and promoted a project manager to COO. With his management team in place, they took on fine-tuning their foundation element. They implemented new HR onboarding protocols and upgraded their accounting system and CRM system. Next, they enhanced their leadership element by promoting some excellent talent, identifying, and nurturing potential high performers, and creating training programs to upgrade their existing staff.

Predictable Profitable Results

Consistent, reliable growth measured in profitability and sales (we call that predicable profitable growth) allows a company to plan and earmark resources for expansion. It creates a foundation upon which great things can happen. It ends the problem of having to figure out what we can cut and what we can keep. Now the focus is on what's next.

This set up consistent growth of 40 percent year-over-year and a continued 20 percent net profitability.

Jack is the "genius CEO" who figured out how to engage all his staff in the company's goals by knowing where to start. Then he showed his team how they could consistently produce the results needed to grow at a healthy, sustainable clip. He showed them new ways of thinking, focusing first on identifying the low hanging fruit on existing jobs (the easy 90 percent). He let the 10 percent hard stuff (attracting new clients) take care of itself over time with a business development hire. He turned his project management team around, making them not just part of the delivery of product/service but also part of the sales force by identifying potential work that only they could know about.

Jack pulled his company out of Transition in one year. He is now ready to be bolder. So what did Jack take on next? He acquired another company to augment his services. He had the confidence in himself and his team to integrate the new company and win big.

Jack is not a unicorn. When our clients engage in the process of finding the right problem to solve, and incorporating it into their strategic lens, 100 percent of them became better. When they took the next step and developed genius thinking not only did they become bigger, but they also became bolder.

So can you.

And, In Closing

In our consulting practice we have seen many CEOs trying to squeeze every last ounce of work from their staff. It is understandable with the cost of doing business going up, particularly in attracting good staff (everything from wage increases to rising health care costs). It is becoming harder and harder to make a profit in today's economic climate. So, business owners often look to get more out of their staff. They call it "increasing productivity". It really means trying to get more output for the same cost. When the staff push back, either through poor morale, absenteeism, or turnover, the CEO thinks, "my people could be better". Shift that thinking.

We have seen the toll it takes on a business owner when that thinking creeps in. It diminishes a positive outlook on the future. It seems to breed increasing problems internally and externally. And it can leave one feeling tired or overwhelmed or maybe not up to the task at hand – feeling like an imposter.

The men and women you have been reading about are not a rare group of extraordinarily talented people with big brains or unusual talent who figured out the secret to driving more productivity. They didn't even have better luck than most. They didn't avoid the pitfalls most of us experience. They are all regular folks who worked hard and were unwilling to do the same thing over and over again expecting a different result. They looked for new ways of thinking that would change the game and the outcome in their favor. In that, each one became extraordinary. Each one became a genius—like Diego, overnight.

Recently, the pandemic provided us all with the opportunity to grow and change. It was a game changer for every business. It was sudden and unexpected. And it was external to your business, so you had no control over it. Companies (and individuals) that pivoted quickly made a lot of money. Those that could not struggled. Set your company up to be able to pivot for the next unexpected thing. It is coming.

We leave you with this.

Ask the right questions. More importantly, solve the right problems. Remember, not all problems need to resolved.

Surround yourself with people who think outside-the-box (genius thinking) to help you be better. Eliminate the noise of all those squeaking wheels demanding your precious attention with unimportant but urgent wants.

Never doubt that you can do this. Yes, you will make mistakes until the day you die. Learn from them fast and it will be worth the time and money the mistake cost. Drag out the learning (which includes not firing staff fast enough) by arguing, blaming or not being responsible and it will cost precious time and money and sometimes even the company. And that will be the real mistake, not the original thing that tripped you up. If you want to minimize your exposure to costly mistakes take on counsel from those who have an unbiased perspective.

You have the strength, courage, and intellect to solve anything that comes your way. How do we know that? Because that's what a leader does. Remember to invest in your staff. They will reward you with loyalty and trust and they will help you fulfill on your dreams—if you let them.

Imagine if you knew every year your company would grow consistently at, for example, 30 percent per year, what else would you do? What else would you be willing to try today? Where else would you focus your time? What would you no longer hesitate to invest in: your people? Your infrastructure? A new product or direction? That is the opportunity you want to create. Start by doing one new thing you learned from this book

Be Better. Bigger. Bolder.

Ready to Put Leadership Into Action? Let's Talk.

If this book inspired you to lead more effectively but you're wondering how to apply these ideas in your organization or personal leadership journey, we'd love to help.

Leaders aren't just born that way. It takes time. If you want to be your best let us help you get there faster...

Go to our website or scan the QR code below to schedule a free discovery session or learn more about how we can work together. You can also reach Rosemary directly at RPaetow@ thinkinstrategy.com.

www.betterbiggerbolder.com

APPENDIX

A   Acknowledgments

From Rosemary

This book could not have been written without the scores of entrepreneurs who entrusted their companies, their creations to me and this process. People like Dan Flood, who grew his organization from $30mm to nearly $100 mm before retiring. George England, who grew his division from $4mm to $50mm. Brian Reduenz, who grew his business from $30mm to $60mm and Adam Weiler, whose company grew from $4mm to $15mm during our tenure. Shane Hunter who had the courage to start his own firm and grew it to $3mm in under 3 years. Sam Brotman who started with us at $2.5mm and is now well over $10mm. And Gary Peterson who started with inStrategy at $1.4mm and earned top dollar when he sold his company. And, of course, all the members of V1274 and V3046 from Vistage.

These are just a few of the many people I've had the honor to walk with on their path. And these people did not just create thriving businesses. They provided opportunities to their staff and gave back to their communities in spades. The courage, determination and heart they exhibited in their process of becoming better, bolder leaders is breathtaking.

This book would not have been possible without the guidance, patience, and persistence of our publishing team. Special thanks to Henry and Devin.

And mostly I want to thank my family, starting with my parents. They came to this country without a penny, barely speaking English and no high school education. They taught me to always strive for my dreams and that anything is possible. My father taught me everything about strategy through tennis: from anticipating, to reading others to winning the mental game (beating those who had better skills but not better thinking). My mother taught me the importance of values. She taught me to do my best, be my best, and deliver more than expected. My brother taught me about teamwork and kindness.

Last and not least are my husband and son. They have always believed in me and encouraged me to be my best. Thank you for trusting me and loving me and knowing that I have more in me than I give myself credit for. My husband knows the right questions to help me dig deeper and understand better the patterns I see. He taught me about flow and design, two essential skills a CEO needs.

My son, Chris taught me three things. The first is anything a person desires is possible. The second is the definition of a leader. The third is what it means to be a mentor. When he was eleven, I wanted to help him make decisions about his future. He kept resisting the idea until I got curious and asked him. I explained how I had a better perspective (my knowledge, experience, and age) than he did. And he agreed that I did. But he was still unwilling to "take my advice". Why? Because, as he put it, I didn't know his purpose, only he did. It was for him to determine his direction, not me. And that is something I take to our clients. Honoring that they are the experts on their path. And we are only here to help them with perspective (not the answer).

Last to my co-author Bob who kept driving for better clarity. This book wouldn't be nearly as good without his input and relentless commitment to excellence.

From Bob Sher

When I first stepped into a leadership role, as a twenty-nine-year-old district supervisor, the regional manager (my manager's manager) said to "always treat people the way you want to be treated." Ben Johnson was a figure straight out of central casting. He was very "John Wayne-esque"—a tall, older gentleman with a big presence from a booming voice. It scared many of us when we had to deal with him, but once I got into leadership, I found that he was the most practical, pragmatic, and caring individual I ever had the chance to work for. He taught me that leadership is about the people and if they feel you have their back, they will do anything for you.

Throughout my career, I've had the privilege of working for and with several outstanding leaders. My criteria for whether a leader is "outstanding" is whether I learned something from them. Along the way, each leader I encountered taught me more about people, the art and science of leadership, and myself. Those lessons, in turn, helped me create my leadership philosophy and style, which is part of what we're trying to impart here. Thank you.

I also want to acknowledge my business partner, Rosemary, for her creativity, insight, and patience. While the bulk of my career has been in the corporate world, she's developed an amazing practice in the leadership development arena. Her superpower is the ability to see through the fog to the root problem that is getting in the way of accomplishing what you are seeking. She openly shared her philosophy, evolved out of many years of working with companies in Transition. Yet she was also open to new ways of looking at things. This allowed us to come up with something much better and more powerful than either of us could have done on our own. This book truly represents the melding of our experiences gained over many years.

Our editor and book coach, Henry Devries, has been a friend for over fifteen years. He falls into the category of "one of the smartest people I know" and that was long before I considered writing a book. He has a unique way of getting you to think creatively, using stories and analogies to draw out the substance in a way that makes it simple for everyone. He's also one of the most patient people I know. He warned us when we started this endeavor that two people writing a book would be exponentially more challenging. He was right. He also said that the journey would take us to places we hadn't even thought of yet. Right again.

Finally, I want to acknowledge my family for their love, support, and patience. Family has often been the "leadership test track", giving me a chance to test drive concepts. I once overheard my older daughter, Stefanie, when she was about twelve, explaining to a friend what her "daddy" did. Stefanie told her young friend that her father was "the boss". The friend asked, "What does the boss do?" Stefanie said that "the boss told people what to do." That reinforced the fact that, while some people perceive leadership as telling people what to do, it really is about creating the time, space, and environment for others to do their best work.

My wife Rhonda also falls into the category of "one of the smartest people I know." Her expertise in social networking, especially LinkedIn, is outstanding. What she's been able to accomplish in her business is an inspiration for what I can accomplish in this chapter of my career. Thank you for believing in me.

B   About The Authors

Rosemary Paetow is the founder and president of Think inStrategy. She brings a rare talent to her clients in the areas of process, performance, and people expertise. First, as a former CPA from KPMG, she is trained to quickly identify a company's key business risk and their areas of constraint (often not obvious). She assesses business processes to determine alignment between strategy and results. A company's efficiency, effectiveness, and viability to scale are quickly revealed. Second, as a former VAR (value added reseller) of accounting systems, she understands how to evaluate and then design systems to support the strategic objectives of a company that enhances performance across the board. Third, with her personal development training she understands how to motivate and inspire staff to produce. And finally, Rosemary has thirteen years of boots on the ground as an employee and manager running departments, executing on strategy, and developing teams to become high performers. She's been in the trenches, so her perspective is based on proven methodologies, not just theoretical concepts.

As a successful owner and manager of a mid-tier accounting software consulting firm for nine years, Rosemary now applies her skillset to train CEOs to become better leaders, to make bigger decisions, and to produce bolder results. Combining the skills attained as a scientist, CPA, and CEO (logic skills of analysis, strategic, and systems thinking) with the soft skills of emotional intelligence (self-awareness), Rosemary helps owners to better motivate managers and employees. She brings a strong financial as well as an OD (organizational development) understanding to her clients. She can be reached at: rpaetow@ thinkinstrategy.com.

Bob Sher is an inStrategist for Think inStrategy. He specializes in the functions of sales, marketing, and operations. Bob brings the perspective of having worked in leadership, management, and executive roles for companies across the spectrum from small to large. He often found himself on the *bleeding edge*, taking mature companies, sometimes kicking and screaming, into new products or services, taking them outside of traditional comfort zones into new markets.

As the West Coast general manager for Tension Corporation, a large envelope manufacturer, Bob led a twenty-four-hour/

seven-day-per-week operation that included over one hundred bargaining unit associates, staff, managers, and salespeople. Among other things, using principles of lean manufacturing, Bob's team was able to reduce cost and waste by shifting thinking from striving for more output to focusing in on the quality of how work was being performed.

For Kinko's (now FedEx Office), Bob created a unique offering for outsourcing that leveraged the footprint of the local Kinko's store to reduce the expense of in-house, on-site services.

As a project manager for Moore Corporation (now RR Donnelley), Bob led a cross functional, inter-company team that resulted in a multi-million-dollar service outsourcing program for one of North America's largest banks.

However, professionally, the thing Bob is proudest of are the people he's led that have gone on to have outstanding careers which they attribute, in part, to his training, mentoring, coaching, and leadership. Bob can be reached at bsher@thinkinstrategy.com.

Cultural Assessment

If you send us your values, we would be happy to do a quick assessment and let you know which culture they fall into based on your description free of charge. Send to rpaetow@thinkinstrategy.com.

WORKS REFERENCED AND NOTES

ENDNOTES

[1] A midsize company has $3 million to $50 million in revenue and between fifteen and one hundred fifty employees. Under $3 million are considered emerging companies.

[2] PM firm is defined as having revenues in excess of ten million dollars in revenue.

[3] One in a thousand startups will get to $10 million in revenue – the bottom threshold of success according to BetterTrainer@ https://bretttrainor.com.

[4] MH Golden Construction (second largest general contractor), Paul Ecke Ranch (the largest poinsettia grower in the world), Continental Maritime (the third largest ship rebuilder).

[5] Kinko's, Tension Envelopes.

[6] Success by our definition is becoming a professionally managed company with consistent, predictable growth.

[7] Oxford English Dictionary, "An arcade game in which players use a mallet to hit toy moles, which appear at random, back into their holes."

[8] Only 5 percent of entrepreneurs ever get out of this mom-and-pop stage. Said another way, 95 percent of business owners fail to achieve their dream business. That means nineteen out of twenty fail to get out of Transition.

[9] Document your business model processes.

[10] Simon Synek, *Start With Why*, (London: Portfolio Co, 2009). It is really good and his book *Leaders Eat Last* is even better.

[11] Buy-in is when you convince the market to buy your product or service. Requires that you expend money (advertising) to push your message out because there is not yet a pull for your product/service.

[12] One way to increase revenue (and profitability) is to increase prices without adding services. When we talk about growth, (scaling) we do not include this in our metrics.

[13] Read Jaynie Smith's book, *Creating your Competitive Advantage* to learn more about this topic.

[14] Former Vistage Chair and author of Creating your Competitive Advantage.

[15] Link to: Things Candidates Want from Employers in 2020: https://www.lever.co/blog/8-things-candidates-want-from-employers-in-2020/.

[16] Malcolm Gladwell, *Outlier* (New York, NY: Little, Brown and CO., 2008).

[17] John W. Bergman, retired US Marine Corps lieutenant general.

[18] www.leadershipfirst.net.

[19] See our Predictable Profitability System on page vii.

[20] 20701_CL_AlignYourLeaders_White-Paper_Nov2018.pdf.

[21] Read Larry Wilson and Hersch Wilson, Play to Win, *Choosing Growth over Fear in Work and Life* (La Vergne, TN: Bard Press, 2004) for more on this great topic.

[22] F. Scott Fitzgerald in his 1936 essay "The Crack-Up."

[23] https://fs.blog/2018/01/complexity-bias/.

[24] Edgar H. Schein, Organizational Culture and Leadership, (Hoboken, NJ: Jossey-Bass, 2017).

[25] Schein, Organizational Culture and Leadership, pg 23.

[26] Nafees Butt, "What do we mean by Culture", medium.com, accessed March 11, 2023, https://medium.com/@Elabor8/the-schneider-culture-model-a-series-8f88c9f00a74.

www.ingramcontent.com/pod-product-compliance
Lightning Source LLC
Chambersburg PA
CBHW031945190326
41519CB00007B/667